GW00993246

Carlo Zella Editore

Toscofolcloristici

1

Our thanks to Roberto Baldini for the images from his archive
and to Paolo Piazzesi for his excellent advice

Front cover:
Silvia Valgiusti's adaptation of a 1935 illustration by Giuseppe Novello: 'Tuscan Cuisine is fine and delicate'

Back cover:
Good luck illustration. From an art nouveau postcard from the A. Sockl series, Vienna

Layout:
Erika Bresci

Originally published as: *Ricette Ignoranti. La Toscana in 100 pietanze "gastronomicamente scorrette"*
1st edition: September 2019
1st reprint: September 2020
2nd reprint: March 2022
1st English edition: February 2024 (translation: Aelmuire Helen Cleary)

© 2024 Leonardo Libri srl
Via Livorno, 8/32 - 50142 Florence - Tel. 055 73787
info@leonardolibri.com - www.leonardolibri.com

ISBN 978-88-88433-40-0

ANDREA GAMANNOSSI   ANTONIO PAGLIAI

Rude Food

*The seamy underbelly of Tuscan cuisine
in 100 'gastronomically incorrect' recipes*

cZ

CARLO ZELLA EDITORE

A book for the erudite in search of the rude!

It would certainly seem that – unless we wish to invoke the evidence of the 'noble savage' – the term 'rude' has precious little to recommend it. The synonyms only reinforce this impression, ranging from rough, raw, crude, and coarse, to primitive, uncouth, ignorant, unrefined, unskilled and ill-mannered, right through to gross, boorish, vulgar, and even offensive. Nevertheless, it's important to have a clear idea of what 'rude food' is, since the whole book revolves around this concept. Eating is perhaps in itself an intrinsically 'rude' activity, because it involves the body in its most primitive, instinctive and uncouth functions. Heralded by activation of the senses of sight, smell, and touch that trigger the production of saliva, food then passes through the mouth. Here, it titillates the taste buds that transmit sensations to the brain, where they merge with experience and olfactory input to produce an emotional and sensory response. After swallowing, the food begins to make its way through the labyrinthine digestive tract, destined eventually to the inexorable (and unmentionable) outcome. Eating is one of the most irrepressible instincts, one of the most basic needs, and however many sophisticated anthropological and cultural constructions we wish – quite rightly – to build upon it, it remains one of the most basic urges that we have in common with other animals. Now, going by this reasoning, all dishes would be rude: steamed bean sprouts would be no less so than tripe with sauce; rather, since the former are less refined, they could even be considered 'ruder'. But the way we see it, a recipe is rude when it is heavy, slightly repugnant, politically incorrect, frowned on by dieticians, belonging to an archaic tradition, spicy, garlicky or in any case strong-flavoured, difficult to digest or perhaps all of these together!

The following six categories of dishes can further enlighten us on all the different 'shades of rudeness'

1. Revolting. For instance, let's take frogs and snails. Or pork blood... Not everyone has the guts to eat such disgusting dishes. Well, this book is aimed in particular at people who do have the guts and are anything but revolted!

 2. Greasy. What can we say? Cholesterol, the fat present in our blood, plays an important role in how our organism works. Several degenerative illnesses involve a build-up of cholesterol components in the tissue. But being aware of this doesn't mean we have to ban from our diet for ever the sausage – or rather the even ruder Florentine *bardiccio* – or the ancient and exquisite *cibréo*. Let's just enjoy them in moderation.

 3. Uncouth. It goes without saying that a good dish of humble tradition, austerely prepared and served in an 'unrefined' way – that is without formal or aesthetic elaboration – constitutes rude food: for instance, a panzanella, served in a typical green 'zangola' bowl that makes it look very much like chicken feed.

 4. Rehashed. In addition to leftover boiled meat reheated in a stew or made into meatballs, we also have stale bread transformed into bread soup and, if there's still some left, ultimately into *ribollita* – remade twice over!

 5. Shameful. This is how we define all the dishes made using offal, giblets, butchers' offcuts, and the less noble or downright unspeakable animal parts such as feet, entrails, poultry combs, tongues, eyeballs, brains and worse. In a word: the nasty bits and the naughty bits.

 6. Unforgettable. These are heavy dishes because they contain meat – maybe raw – the digestion of which, as we know, engages our body for several hours. Dishes that leave a foul-smelling memory in the mouth because they are laden with garlic or onions, or peppers or radishes; legume-based dishes that blow us up like balloons. These and other recipes generating undesirable consequences are the stars of the last and rudest category of all.

Then there are dishes disguised by a false propriety, concealing under demure and graceful names recipes that would make even a trucker blush. For instance, the delicacy that goes by the deceptively elegant moniker of *francesina*, which is made with leftover boiled meat, two kilos of red onions, meat stock, and lashings of olive oil: you never can trust a name!

Illustration taken from the frontispiece of *Annulaire agathopédique et saugial* 'imprimé par les presses iconographiques a la Congrève de l'Ordre des Agath., chez A. Labroue et Compagnie, rue de la Fourghe, 36, a Bruxelles.'

Or the aforementioned *cibrèo* belonging to category 2 (*greasy*), which – being made of chicken livers, hearts, combs, wattles, and testicles – is indisputably *shameful* (5) and also *revolting* (1): a perfect example of the multifariously rude!

And so, we have devised a 'rudeness index' from 1 to 6, marking each recipe with a number of boar's heads equivalent to the number of rude categories that the dish manages to notch up: from 0 for the 'politically correct' recipes – notable by their complete absence – up to a grand total of 6 for those that can be defined as revolting *and* greasy *and* uncouth *and* rehashed *and* shameful *and* unforgettable. These particular delicacies are guaranteed to immediately make any prig, woke warrior, radical liberal, animal rights activist, vegan, or dietician pass out on the spot. To make it easier to find what you're looking for, we have chosen to organise the recipes in courses, dividing them into four categories from starters to dessert, with the dishes numbered from 1 to 100. We have also indicated the province of Tuscany that each recipe comes from. Some are to be found in only one particular place – such as the famous stuffed celery from Prato – whereas for others there are variants even outside Tuscany, for instance the tripe in sauce eaten in Rome is not very different from our own. Obviously, the same recipe can feature quite considerable variations between one province and another, or between one district and another, or even between families in the same district! Sometimes we can find the same recipe in two places, where it is known by different names, or again two totally different recipes with the same name. All this is the result of the extraordinary historic and cultural richness of Tuscany, or we could even say of Italy as a whole. And it is also the result of a national unification that has never completely taken place. Details of these and other gastronomic variants, as well as anecdotes and history related to the dishes, will be provided in notes in italics at the end of the recipes, albeit without weighing them down since the gastronomical matter is already heavy enough in itself! Clearly, there are also quite a number of terms related to the ingredients that cannot be translated into English, for instance cuts of meat or methods of processing cheeses and sausages that are not equivalent between culinary cultures. For these too we provide explanatory notes, possible alternatives, and the suggestion that sometimes the preparation of the dish in question may have to be postponed until the next visit to Tuscany!

So, where did the idea for this book come from? From a meeting between two people. A writer who made his name in the thriller genre and over time developed an interest in gastronomy and struck up a friendship with a publisher-foodie who was passionate about Tuscan cuisine. They were both rather fed up with the boring and anaemic dishes proposed by the new culinary trends and decided to go all out for something reactionary. Actually, it was hard to understand why no one had thought of it before! A cookery book written by two men, crammed with recipes for rude food might appear to be targeted at a male public. Far from it! Most of our recipes were traditionally prepared by women, because only they were able to give that delicate touch to dishes that had very little of delicate about them. Nor do we want the book to be seen as a species of *In Praise of Rudeness*, since we have used the term 'rude' affectionately to refer to an uncouth, inelegant and heavy cuisine, fully aware at the same time that behind every one of these recipes there is an ancient and deeply entrenched culture. Consequently, we believe that this book can offer today's 'erudite' food lovers the chance

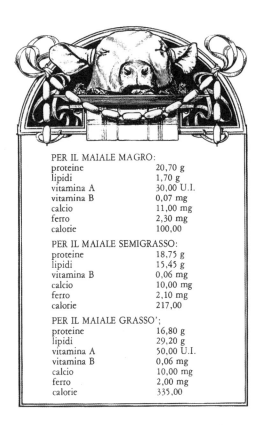

PER IL MAIALE MAGRO:	
proteine	20,70 g
lipidi	1,70 g
vitamina A	30,00 U.I.
vitamina B	0,07 mg
calcio	11,00 mg
ferro	2,30 mg
calorie	100,00

PER IL MAIALE SEMIGRASSO:	
proteine	18,75 g
lipidi	15,45 g
vitamina B	0,06 mg
calcio	10,00 mg
ferro	2,10 mg
calorie	217,00

PER IL MAIALE GRASSO';	
proteine	16,80 g
lipidi	29,20 g
vitamina A	50,00 U.I.
vitamina B	0,06 mg
calcio	10,00 mg
ferro	2,00 mg
calorie	335,00

List of the nutrients contained in 100 g of pork.

to courageously try their hand at recipes they have never heard of and don't know how to prepare, in the conviction that in this delightfully rude food they will discover amazing flavours that they could never have imagined.

Below you will find a 'rudography': a short list of the books that immediately come to mind when addressing the issue of rude food. Starting with the classics, the *Re dei Cuochi* contains recipes so drenched in fat as to make a Big Mac seem Lenten fare, as underscored in the recent book by G. Coppetti *Così mangiavano e ridevano i nostri nonni*. This is followed by *La scienza in cucina*, whose author – the famous Pellegrino Artusi – for instance, recommends garnishing your just-cooked Florentine beefsteak with a hefty knob of butter. Artusi also places at the end of his book an appendix devoted to suggestions for those with weak stomachs, which would appear to be an estimable and extremely modern consideration were it not for the fact that the proposed dishes are unspeakably rude: e.g. fried testicles, sweetbread croquettes, and stuffed cutlets!

Trionfo su 'l gran fianco Ercole avvinto
Lo spoglio de l'ucciso empio leone.
Io, portando su 'l dorso un porco estinto,
Vuo' trionfar de l'uccisor d'Adone.
21

Etching from 1660 by Giuseppe Maria Mitelli (1634–1718) showing a 'pig porter', copy from the *Arti di Bologna* by Annibale Carracci (1560-1609). Inscription: *Trionfò su 'l gran fianco Ercole avvinto/ lo spoglio de l'ucciso empio leone./ Io, portando su 'l dorso un porco estinto/ Vuo' trionfar de l'uccisor d'Adone.*

A tavola apparecchiata by A. Bencistà deals exclusively with traditional rude food, by way of example *ciccoli* or cracklings, dried pieces of pork fat that are by-products of lard processing. *La Bibbia della trippa* – a masterpiece of the most erudite rude cuisine from the very heart of Tuscany – could be subtitled 'Everything you ever wanted to know about entrails but were ashamed to ask'. *Cucina del cuore della Toscana*, penned by two chefs experienced in the preparation of record-breaking mega-banquets, presents 300 succulent and nutritious recipes from the finest regional tradition.

In his *Ricette proibite*, Tebaldo Lorini has said all there is to be said about the types of flesh permitted or forbidden in various civilisations, about the seamy underbelly of cuisine that outrages and offends animal rights activists, and about what we all find disconcerting, and why.

In short, a book that explores at depth what man is and what animals are, but also a journey into the past when we even ate cats and mice to survive, at a time when food really was incontrovertibly rude!

RUDOGRAPHY

Con poco o nulla. Ricette di cucina popolare toscana, ed. by C. Costantini, LEF, Florence 2004.

*Cucina toscana. Ricette per ghiottoni e buongustai.*Vol. 2, LEF, Florence 2005.

Pellegrino Artusi, *La scienza in cucina e l'arte di mangiar bene*, Sarnus, Florence 2010.

ROBERTO BALDINI, ALFREDO SCANZANI, *La Bibbia della trippa. Ricette, storie e curiosità sulle frattaglie*, Sarnus, Florence 2015.

ALESSANDRO BENCISTÀ, *A tavola apparecchiata. I custodi della tradizione nella cucina quotidiana: dal fattore Oliviero a Nonna Giuditta*, Sarnus, Florence 2015.

ALESSANDRO BENCISTÀ, *Il maiale dall'Arista allo Zampone. Con un'antologia letteraria in prosa e in rima e la versione integrale de L'Eccellenza et trionfo del porco di Giulio Cesare Croce*, Polistampa, Florence 2007.

CARLA GERI CAMPORESI, *Ceci, fagioli, lenticchie*, Maria Pacini Fazzi, Lucca 1999.

CARLA GERI CAMPORESI, *Ricette Tradizionali Fiorentine*, Maria Pacini Fazzi, Lucca 2007.

GIANFRANCO COPPETTI, *Così mangiavano e ridevano i nostri nonni. Ricette d'altri tempi… e non solo*, Sarnus, Florence 2017.

MARIA CONCETTA FOZZER, *La Cucina del giorno dopo*, Sarnus, Florence 2011.

ANDREA GAMANNOSSI, *Le ricette d'amore della nonna*, Sarnus, Florence 2015.

ANDREA GAMANNOSSI, *La Toscana dal bosco alla cucina*, Sarnus, Florence 2012.

LICIA LARI, MAURO MONTANELLI, *Cucina del cuore della Toscana. Con uno sguardo a quella degli antenati. Curiosità, tradizioni e oltre 300 ricette*, Sarnus, Florence 2005.

TEBALDO LORINI, *Ricette proibite. Rane, asini, rondinotti, gatti e tartarughe nella tradizione alimentare*, Sarnus, Florence 2012.

INES MUGNAI, CRISTINA MANNELLI, ELENA GALEOTTI, *Cucina nostrale*, LEF, Florence 2006.

GIOVANNI NELLI, *Il re dei cuochi. Trattato di gastronomia universale*, Legros Felice, Milano 1868.

PAOLO PIAZZESI, *Dizionario enogastronomico della Toscana*, Nardini, Florence 2007.

LUCIA PUGLIESE, *Il lampredotto salverà l'euro*, Il Pozzo di Micene, Florence 2012.

LAURA RANGONI, *La povera nobiltà della trippa*, Maria Pacini Fazzi, Lucca 2000.

A few notes on cheeses and sausages

In addition to the ubiquitous Parmesan, Grana Padana *and* Mozzarella *that we all know and love, the other cheeses mentioned in the recipes are* Abbucciato *and* Caciotta *(see recipe 23) and, most important of all,* Pecorino. *Pecorino Toscano is a hard sheep's milk cheese more popularly known simply as 'cacio'. It has been produced in Tuscany since at least the time of Pliny the Elder and, it would appear, was even made by the Etruscans.*

Pancetta *and* Lardo *are other ingredients used in several recipes.* Pancetta *is salt-cured pork belly and, although there is no real equivalent, it can if necessary be replaced with green bacon. For* Lardo, *or fatback, see recipe 14. Then there are the sausages:* Mortadella *is made from finely ground pork incorporating small pieces of fat and whole black peppercorns, or sometimes pistachios. The most famous Mortadella comes from Bologna, but the Mortadella from Prato is also greatly appreciated.* Finocchiona *is a typical Tuscan sausage made with fennel seeds and red wine, while the unquestionably ruder* Soprassata *is an uncured Tuscan sausage made with leftover pig parts including head, skin and tongue (see recipe 54).*

The quantities in all recipes are calculated for four persons, except where otherwise indicated.
The olive oil used in the recipes is always extra virgin olive oil, preferably Tuscan!
As known, Tuscan bread is always unsalted.

STARTERS AND SAUCES

Previous page: a satirical vignette by Giuseppe Novello, from *Il signore di buona famiglia* (Mondadori 1942). 'Family boarding house from 20 lire upwards … The 20 lire boarder has already finished.'

1.
Acciugata – *Anchovy Paste*
Florence / Livorno / Grosseto

Ingredients:

6 salted anchovies
1 clove garlic
olive oil

Wash and bone the anchovies under running water.
Put four tablespoons of olive oil and the peeled and squashed garlic clove in a saucepan.
Add the anchovy fillets and cook over a low heat stirring until they have dissolved.
Remove the garlic clove.
This paste can be used to prepare crostini with slices of buttered toast.

This sauce was widely used in the past too. The ancient Romans made a spicier version that they called 'garum'. It is also made in several areas of Umbria.
Anchovy paste is very versatile and can also be used as a sauce for pasta or as an accompaniment to boiled meat or fish. It is also delicious on fried pork chops or with chicory.

2.

Acciughe sotto il pesto - *Anchovies in Pesto*
Livorno / Grosseto

Ingredients:

> 300 g salted anchovies
> olive oil
> parsley
> garlic
> chilli pepper
> boiled potatoes

Wash the anchovies under cold running water and remove the bones taking care not to split the fillets.

Finely chop the garlic, parsley and chilli pepper.

Place the anchovies in a dish, covering each layer with the chopped garlic mixture and a trickle of olive oil.

Serve with boiled potatoes in deep bowls.

Alternatively, fresh anchovies can also be prepared 'alla povera', that is, accompanied simply with chopped onions and vinegar.

3.

Alici ripiene - *Stuffed Anchovies*

Massa Carrara / Livorno / Pisa

Ingredients:

600 g fresh anchovies
bread without crusts soaked in milk
groundnut oil for frying
2 eggs
garlic
parsley
grated Parmesan cheese
salt
chilli pepper

Wash about 500 g of anchovies (choosing the thinner ones) and open them by pulling the head towards the tail on the belly side, removing the innards. Be careful not to completely split the two fillets, but if you do, just add the fish flesh to the filling.

To make the filling, mash the remaining 100 g of anchovies and mix thoroughly with the bread soaked in milk, one whole egg, the grated Parmesan cheese, the chopped garlic and parsley, ground chilli pepper, and salt to taste. Use a teaspoon to spread the filling on the open anchovies and then close them again. If you wish, tie them with kitchen string to prevent them opening. Gently coat them in flour and dip in the beaten egg, then fry in plenty of hot oil. The anchovies can be served like this, browned and fried, or heated up again in a tomato sauce flavoured with wild fennel.

Anchovies, or 'acciughe' – also known as 'alici' in Italian – are considered humble fare and are rarely found on modern restaurant menus. In actual fact, they are extremely tasty and suitable for numerous dishes. Being oily fish, they are also rich in omega-3 fatty acids.

4.

Chioccioline di mare piccanti - *Spicy Whelks*
Livorno / Massa Carrara / Grosseto

Ingredients:

> 1 kg whelks
> 500 g peeled tomatoes
> garlic
> white wine
> olive oil
> chilli pepper
> salt

Soak the whelks in brine for a couple of hours and then wash them.

Squash two garlic cloves with the heel of your hand and put them in a frying pan with a little oil.

As soon as the garlic begins to colour, tip in the whelks, then pour over half a glass of white wine and let it evaporate.

Add the peeled tomatoes cut into chunks and a generous pinch of chilli pepper.

Cook for a good half hour or until the sauce has thickened.

To get the whelks out of their shells you can use a toothpick or adopt the decidedly ruder approach of simply sucking them out!

5.

Cozze ripiene alla versiliese - *Versilia Stuffed Mussels*
Massa Carrara / Lucca

Ingredients:

12 large mussels or 16 smaller ones
70 g tuna in oil
2 eggs
2 tablespoons of grated Grana Padana cheese
garlic
400 g peeled tomatoes
150 g breadcrumbs
parsley
salt and pepper
olive oil

Mix together the drained and chopped tuna, breadcrumbs, cheese and eggs and season with salt and pepper.
Clean and rinse the mussels, removing the beard, then open them with the help of a knife.
Fill the mussels with the mixture, then close them again and tie them with kitchen string.
Put two tablespoons of oil, the chopped parsley and the chopped tomatoes into a frying pan with the two unpeeled garlic cloves.
Cook for about ten minutes, then add the stuffed mussels and continue cooking for another ten minutes.
Tip into a serving dish and serve with a sprinkle of chopped fresh parsley.

In some versions the tuna is replaced with chopped Mortadella sausage, which is made from finely ground pork incorporating small pieces of fat and whole black peppercorns, or sometimes pistachios. This gives the mussels an unusual flavour that is very pleasant on the palate.

6.

Crostini all'aretina - *Arezzo Crostini*

Arezzo

Ingredients:

200 g Tuscan bread or a bread stick
200 g rabbit liver
150 g chicken breast
1 onion
1 egg yolk
1 tablespoon capers
bread crumb
stock
white wine
mixed pickled vegetables
vinegar
olive oil
salt and pepper
150 g Scarpaccia ham

> *A note on 'crostini' and 'crostoni'*
> *Here and in the following recipes you will find the words both 'crostini' and 'crostoni'.*
> *Both words are formed with the same noun but they have diminutive and augmentative suffixes respectively – namely 'ini' and 'oni'.*
> *To put it less eruditely and more rudely: we're talking about a little slice and a big slice!*

Chop the chicken breast into chunks and finely chop the onion. Tip both into a saucepan with two tablespoons of olive oil, sauté gently until golden then leave to cook for about ten minutes. Add the chopped rabbit liver, moisten with white wine and continue cooking for another ten minutes.

Chop everything together then tip it back into the saucepan, add the stock, the egg yolk, the capers, a piece of bread crumb soaked in vinegar and two tablespoons of chopped pickled vegetables.

Season with salt and pepper and complete the cooking, adding more stock if required.

Spread the paste on slices of bread stick or Tuscan bread.

Serve accompanied by a tray of Scarpaccia ham.

Scarpaccia cured ham is considered one of the best in Tuscany, and even beyond!

7.

Crostini di fegatini alla pistoiese con arista sott'olio
Pistoia Liver Crostini with Pork Loin
Pistoia

Ingredients:

500 g chicken liver
4 anchovy fillets
2 handfuls salted capers
1 small onion
½ glass vin santo (or dessert wine)
toasted Tuscan bread
olive oil – salt

First, wash and thoroughly clean the chicken livers, then chop them. Sweat the finely chopped onion gently in a saucepan with a little oil, then add the chopped livers and a just a touch of salt and cook until they are nicely browned but not hard. Pour over the vin santo and let it evaporate. Meanwhile, chop the capers and the anchovy fillets. When the livers are cooked, tip them into a blender with the capers and anchovies and blend to a creamy consistency. Toast the slices of Tuscan bread and spread the paste on top. The crostini can be accompanied by pork loin preserved in oil.

8.

Arista sott'olio – *Pork Loin in Oil*
Pistoia

This starter is a typical Pistoia dish, although the practice of preserving meat in oil is not restricted to this area and was widespread in the past before technology came to our aid. The pork loin is sliced and each slice is covered with a finely chopped mixture of spices and herbs: rosemary, sage, nutmeg, cloves, garlic, pepper and salt. The slices are then rolled up and cooked in lard or pig fat, with a little white wine added. When cooked, the pork slices are stored in oil in vacuum sealed jars for at least a month. But remember … anticipation is the best sauce!

9.

Crostini di beccaccia – *Woodcock Crostini*
Prato / Pistoia / Arezzo

Ingredients:

innards of 2 woodcocks
2 salted anchovies
1 tablespoon chopped parsley
1 tablespoon desalted capers
½ glass dry vin santo (or dry sherry)
20 g butter
olive oil
salt and pepper
slices of Tuscan bread

Bone the anchovies and rinse the capers in cold water, then finely chop both along with the innards.
Melt the butter in a saucepan, then add oil until the bottom is entirely covered. Heat the pan and then add the chopped ingredients.
Sauté gently for a few minutes then season with salt and pepper.
Pour in the vin santo and let it evaporate.
Cut each slice of bread into four then toast them and spread with the paste while it is still hot.

It is not easy to find woodcock for sale, and they are a tasty and sought-after prey for hunters.

10.

Crostini di cinghiale in dolceforte
Sweet and Sour Wild Boar Crostini

Grosseto

Ingredients:

sliced Tuscan bread
500 g well-hung wild boar meat
50 g dark chocolate
20 g sugar
4 crumbled walnuts
20 g steeped raisins
red wine vinegar
meat stock
1 glass red wine
1 glass grappa (or apple or pear brandy)
half an onion, half a carrot and half a stalk of celery
nutmeg
vegetable stock
olive oil – salt and pepper

Finely chop the onion, carrot and celery and sweat gently in a saucepan with three tablespoons of olive oil. Add the chopped boar meat and continue to sauté, then sprinkle with grated nutmeg and season with salt and pepper. Cook for about half an hour then add a glass of red wine and one of vegetable stock. Cover the pan and cook for another hour. Remove the meat, leave it to cool and skim the sauce to remove excess fat. Chop the meat and tip it back into the saucepan. Put a tablespoon of vinegar, the sugar, the glass of grappa, the crumbled walnuts, the flaked chocolate and the drained raisins into a bowl. Mix thoroughly and then tip into the saucepan with the meat and cook for another five minutes. Prepare the crostini with the Tuscan bread and spread the wild boar sauce over them while it is still hot.

11.

Crostini con fegatini di pollo e di coniglio
Chicken and Rabbit Liver Crostini
Arezzo

Ingredients:

> 200 g chicken liver
> 200 g rabbit liver
> 1 onion
> stock
> 2 desalted anchovy fillets
> 1 tablespoon capers
> white wine
> Tuscan bread
> olive oil
> salt and pepper

Chop the onion finely and sauté it in a saucepan with two tablespoons of oil. Add the anchovy fillets and the capers. Tip in the chopped liver and pour over half a glass of white wine, let it evaporate and add a drop of stock. Season with salt and pepper.

Cook for fifteen minutes, then tip the mixture onto a board and chop it finely, then put it back in the saucepan. Alternatively, you can whiz the mixture in a blender.

Cook for another five minutes or until you have a thick consistency.

Slice the bread, then cut the slices in two and dip them in the stock.

Spread the sauce on the crostini while it is still hot.

12.
Crostini maremmani – *Maremma Crostini*
Grosseto

Ingredients:

1 onion
1 carrot
1 celery stalk
1 sprig of rosemary
2 sage leaves
1 clove garlic
2 tablespoons olive oil
300 g chicken liver
1 rabbit liver
100 g pork
sliced Tuscan bread
salt and pepper

Finely chop the onion, celery, rosemary, carrot, sage leaves and garlic. Warm the oil in a saucepan and sauté the chopped vegetables and herbs.

In the meantime, clean the stringy tissue off the livers, then chop them into small pieces. Chop the pork into small pieces too and tip everything into the saucepan. Sauté the meat and vegetable mixture then season with salt and pepper. Leave to cook for about another 20 minutes, adding a little hot stock if required.

Whiz the mixture in the blender, then spread the paste on slices of toasted bread.

13.

Crostini di milza – *Spleen Crostini*
Siena

Ingredients:

500 g calf spleen
½ onion
3 salted anchovy fillets
1 glass red wine
stock
Tuscan bread
50 g butter
olive oil
salt and pepper

Beat the spleen to pulp using the back of a large knife.
Chop the onion finely and sweat in a casserole with the butter and two tablespoons of oil.
Add the spleen, season with salt and pepper and cook, adding the wine gradually. When the wine has evaporated, add the boned anchovy fillets and the chopped capers and continue cooking until you have a smooth consistency.
Slice and toast the bread, then moisten one side of each slice with stock and spread the spleen paste on the other.

14.

Crostoni al lardo - *Lardo Crostoni*
Massa Carrara

Ingredients:

350 g Tuscan bread – preferably baked in a wood-fired oven
180 g lardo
olive oil – preferably from the Lucca hills
black pepper

Cut the bread into twelve slices and toast them on a rack over a bed of coals.
If you don't have a bed of coals to hand, you can just toast them in the oven!
When the toast is ready, place strips of lardo on top of each slice.
Place on a tray (preferably heated) and finish off the crostoni with a twist of
black pepper and a trickle of freshly pressed extra virgin olive oil.

Lardo – not to be confused with lard – is the part of fat taken from the neck and back
of the pig (fatback), and also gives its name to the cured fat made from it, which is
usually served in thin strips.
The most famous is the lardo from Colonnata, a small village in the marble quarries
close to Carrara. Here the lardo is cured for around six months in basins made of
Carrara marble, which are filled with layers of fat seasoned with a mixture of herbs
and spices, garlic, salt, and pepper.

15.

Crostoni di pane al cavolo nero - *Tuscan Kale Crostoni*
Lucca / Florence / Siena

Ingredients (for 8):

500 g leaves Tuscan kale
8 slices of toasted bread
garlic
olive oil
salt and pepper

Boil the kale in a pot of salted water.
Toast the bread directly over the embers, if possible, otherwise the oven will do. Place the toast slices in the serving dishes and rub the upper side with a peeled garlic clove.
Place the kale leaves on the bread, adding a little of the cooking juice, and finish off the crostoni with a twist of black pepper and a trickle of freshly pressed extra virgin olive oil.

Tuscan kale can also be used raw. It can be chopped up with pine nuts, garlic, and mature pecorino cheese to make a type of pesto that can be spread on toast or used as a sauce for pasta.

16.
Crostoni alla salsiccia - *Sausage Crostoni*
Siena / Arezzo / Lucca

Ingredients:

4 sausages, crumbled
250 g fresh Pecorino cheese
Tuscan bread

Cut the Pecorino into small pieces and mix it up with the crumbled sausage meat.
Spread the paste on slices of Tuscan bread cut in half.
Bake in a pre-heated oven at 180°C for a few minutes.

In some modern versions of this recipe the Pecorino cheese is replaced with Stracchino – a soft, creamy cheese made from cow's milk – which gives the crostoni a more delicate flavour.

17.

Fagioli con i ciccioli - *Beans with Cracklings*
Lucca / Florence / Pisa / Siena

Ingredients:

300 g boiled cannellini beans
100 g pork cracklings
2 cloves garlic
sage
1 onion
stock
olive oil
salt and pepper

Gently sweat the finely chopped onion in a saucepan with three tablespoons of olive oil, and then add the cracklings and cook for around 15 minutes, adding stock as required.

Heat up the boiled beans in a little stock with garlic and sage. Drain the beans and tip them into a tureen with the cracklings.

Season with salt and pepper, trickle over extra virgin olive oil and mix delicately.

Serve with another few twists of black pepper.

Ciccioli, like cracklings, are simply pieces of pork fat that are by-products of lard processing. They are then cooked slowly to melt the fat and let the water evaporate, after which they are squeezed between cloths to dry completely to make them keep for longer.

18.
Fagioli saltati con pomodorini
Sautéed Beans with Cherry Tomatoes
Florence / Prato

Ingredients:

250 g boiled cannellini beans
200 g cherry tomatoes
olive oil
salt and pepper

Chop the tomatoes into pieces and place them in a colander to drain.
Heat up plenty of extra virgin olive oil in a frying pan and sauté the beans and the chopped tomatoes for a few minutes, then season with salt and pepper.
Serve piping hot.

This is a very unusual dish that was most common in rustic cooking. The process involved is not actual frying, but the end result is extremely tasty and out of the ordinary.

19.

Fiori fritti all'acciughe – *Fried Zucchini Flowers with Anchovies*
Arezzo / Siena / Florence

Ingredients:

12 zucchini flowers
12 salted anchovy fillets
1 egg
100 g flour
white wine
2 tablespoons olive oil
corn oil for frying
salt and pepper

Put the flour in a bowl with the olive oil, the yolk of the egg, salt, and pepper. Add white wine and water and mix until you have a smooth batter.
Beat the egg white until it is stiff.
Clean the zucchini flowers, removing the pistil and the stalk, and stuff them with the anchovy fillets rinsed under running water.
Add the beaten egg white to the batter and fold in gently.
Drop the flowers into the batter and leave for a few minutes then take them out, drain and deep fry in very hot corn oil.
Serve on plates lined with absorbent paper.

Zucchini flowers can also be filled with other ingredients. In some places even Pecorino cheese is used. They are also excellent without any filling.

20.
Marinelle piccanti al pomodoro - *Spicy Snails in Tomato Sauce*
Florence

Ingredients:

60 g purged 'Marinelle' snails
150 g tomato sauce
1 clove garlic
half an onion
parsley
chilli pepper
olive oil
salt

Gently sweat the chopped onion, garlic, parsley and chilli pepper in a saucepan with five tablespoons of oil until soft.

Tip in the purged snails and cover them with hot water. Reduce the water over a slow heat and then add the tomato sauce.

Season with salt and cook for about two and a half hours, adding more hot water if required.

Serve with an extra sprinkle of powdered chilli pepper.

This is a dish typical of the Florentine suburb of Sesto Fiorentino: the 'Marinelle' snails used – Eobania vermiculata, common name: chocolate-band snail – are harvested on the slopes of the Calvana mountain range.
Snails have to go through a lengthy purging process before cooking, but nowadays it is very easy to find them ready to cook.

21.

Panzerotti golosi – *Greedy Panzerotti*
Florence / Pistoia

Ingredients:

250 g flour
1 glass warm water
1 sachet instant sourdough powder
1 knob of butter
milk
olive oil
sunflower oil for frying
salt

For the filling:

250 g Mozzarella
100 g cooked ham

Prepare the dough by mixing together the flour, sourdough powder, warm water, a drop of milk, a knob of butter and a pinch of salt. Knead well, form into a ball and leave to rise for about an hour.
Roll out the dough and cut out circles of about the size of a saucer.
Place the diced Mozzarella and the sliced ham in the middle then close them up, taking care to seal them well.
Fry in plenty of hot sunflower oil and serve piping hot.

Instant sourdough powder can now be found in some grocery shops and supermarkets. Otherwise, you can substitute brewer's yeast.
For an even more tasty alternative, you can replace the Mozzarella cheese with Pecorino and the cooked ham with Tuscan cured ham.

22.
Roventini - *Pig's Blood Pancakes*
Florence / Prato / Pisa

Ingredients:

    600 cl fresh pig's blood
    2 tablespoons flour
    lard
    salt
    grated Parmesan cheese

Dissolve the flour in a little water and add the blood. Mix well and then season with salt.
Heat it up in a double boiler – or in a bowl over a pot of boiling water – and then set aside for half an hour.
Melt a little lard (or alternatively butter) in a non-stick or cast-iron frying pan. When it is completely hot, pour on a ladleful of the blood batter and cook the pancake on both sides.
Serve immediately, piping hot, with a generous sprinkle of grated Parmesan cheese.

This recipe is the simplest one and the most popular. There are numerous variants, including the sweet version also known as Migliacci, served sprinkled with sugar or sometimes chocolate.

23.
Sformato all'abbucciato – *Abbucciato Souffle*
Arezzo

Ingredients:

100 g Abbucciato cheese
50 g medium mature Tuscan Pecorino DOP
50 g Caciotta cheese
3 eggs
butter to grease the baking dish or moulds
breadcrumbs
salt

For the bechamel sauce:

50 g butter
50 g flour
500 cl milk

Grate the Pecorino and chop the Abbucciato and Caciotta into small pieces. Prepare the bechamel sauce: in a small saucepan melt the butter over a moderate heat, then add the flour stirring thoroughly to avoid lumps forming, then pour in the cold milk all in one go and continue to stir until it starts to boil, season with salt to taste. Continue cooking the bechamel over a low heat for at least twenty minutes, gradually adding the cheeses. Mix everything together well. Then add the egg yolks one at a time, stirring all the time. Beat the egg whites until they are stiff and then fold gently into the cheese sauce. Adjust salt to taste and add a pinch of pepper. Pour the mixture into a buttered baking dish or individual ramekins, and sprinkle the breadcrumbs on top. Bake in a pre-heated oven at 180°C for 20-30 minutes.

Abbucciato is a cheese typical of the Casentino area. It takes its name from the characteristic appearance of the outer rind when it is mature. This particular cheese, which is made using unpasteurised milk from sheep left free to graze, was produced by the Camaldoli monks as far back as the eleventh century. It has a very distinctive flavour, sweet and velvety with a slightly bitter note. Caciotta is a fresh mild-flavoured cheese, made mostly from cow's milk.

24.
Torta d'erbi della Lunigiana "Scarpazza"
Lunigiana Wild Greens Pie
Massa Carrara / Lucca

Ingredients:

1 kg spinach and chard
500 g seasonal wild greens (borage, pimpernel, chicory etc.)
2 leeks
2 zucchini
2 eggs
50 g grated Pecorino cheese
300 g flour
olive oil – salt and pepper

Wash all the vegetables and boil them in salted water, then drain, squeeze and chop them. Tip into a bowl with the Pecorino, the eggs and four table-spoons of oil. Mix well and season with salt and pepper. Prepare the pastry by mixing the flour with four tablespoons of oil, a little salt and about one and a half glasses of water. Knead well then roll the pastry out into two sheets, one larger than the other. Grease a square baking tin and place the larger sheet in it, spoon in the filling and then place the other sheet of pastry on top and pinch the edges together. Bake in a pre-heated oven at 190°C for around half an hour. Can also be served cold.

FIRST COURSES

Previous page: a satirical vignette by Giuseppe Novello, from *Il signore di buona famiglia* (Mondadori 1942). 'The paternal veto … So far papa has not realised that Franceschina has cut her hair in a pageboy'.

25.
Acquacotta con pecorino piccante
Tomato and Onion soup with Pecorino and Poached Eggs
Grosseto / Arezzo / Siena

Ingredients:

4 slices of Tuscan bread
2 onions
500 g peeled tomatoes
4 eggs
vegetable stock
grated mature Pecorino cheese
basil
olive oil
salt and pepper

Sweat the chopped onions in a large saucepan in four tablespoons of oil.
Add the peeled tomatoes and the basil, then season with salt and pepper.
Cook for around 20-25 minutes, then pour in one and a half litres of vege-
table stock and continue cooking for another 30 minutes.
Toast the bread slices. Place one in each bowl and sprinkle with the grated
Pecorino, then ladle the soup over them. Last of all, break an egg carefully
into each dish, making sure it stays whole.

*This is a very humble dish which used to be made by the charcoal makers and the
transhumant shepherds who wandered the country roads. There are numerous versions
of it that vary from one district to another.*

26.
Brodo col centopelle - *Omasum Soup*
Florence / Pistoia

Ingredients:

> 350 g of omasum (a compartment of the stomach, or tripe)
> 60 g pancetta (or green bacon)
> 1 carrot
> 1 onion
> 1 celery stalk
> 100 g Savoy cabbage
> ½ glass tomato conserve
> grated Parmesan cheese
> olive oil
> salt and pepper

Chop the carrot, onion, celery and pancetta and sauté in a large saucepan with four tablespoons of oil.

Add the omasum cut into strips and allow the flavours to blend for a few minutes. Add the cabbage cut into thin strips and the tomato conserve diluted in a little water.

Season with salt and pepper and continue cooking for 15 minutes.

Add one and a half litres of boiling water to cover all the ingredients and cook for around 40 minutes without the lid on.

Serve the soup piping hot with grated Parmesan cheese.

The centopelle, or omasum, is a part of the stomach that is white with numerous 'leaflets'. In other parts of Tuscany it is called 'millefoglie'. It has many very evocative names in English too. As well as the more scientific 'omasum', it is also known as the manyplies, the psalterium, the bible, and the fardel!

27.
Carcerato pistoiese – *Prisoners' Soup*
Pistoia

Ingredients:

400 g stale bread
1 onion
1 celery stalk
1 carrot
3 cherry tomatoes
300 g beef offal (calf's head, trotter, tail, omasum, reticulum, cow's uterus etc.)
grated Pecorino or Parmesan cheese
olive oil
salt and pepper

In a large saucepan prepare a stock with water, the onion, carrot, celery, to-matoes and offal. Cook it for a long time then sieve it. Pour the stock into a pot (preferably earthenware) and add the bread cut into slices, season with salt and pepper and cook over a low heat, stirring all the time until you have a smooth consistency. When it is ready, garnish with a trickle of oil and plenty of cheese. Serve in bowls while it is still piping hot.

This very ancient and typical Tuscan recipe is linked in particular to the city of Pistoia. Its name derives from the fact that in Pistoia the city slaughterhouses were very close to the prison, and both buildings overlooked a small stream called the Brana. It seems that many years ago the entrails or offal of the butchered animals were not sold but were thrown into the stream. Seeing this, the evidently starving prisoners asked whether they could have all these delicacies to eat, and they were given permission. And so, the prisoners invented a soup by cooking the offal together with their rations of dry bread and water. This very humble dish, which nowadays is enhanced by the addition of vegetables and cheese, can also be sa-voured in some trattorias and restaurants. The same recipe is also made in Lucca. Speaking of humble food, the English expression 'humble pie' actually comes from a recipe made using 'umbles', namely the heart, liver, kidneys and lungs of the animal!

28.
Linguine ai ricci di mare - *Linguine with Sea Urchin Sauce*
Livorno / Massa Carrara

Ingredients:

> 350 g pasta (linguine)
> about 30 very fresh sea urchins
> olive oil
> onion
> garlic
> chilli pepper
> 250 ml fish stock
> 300 g peeled tomatoes (roughly chopped)
> parsley
> salt

Cut all round the circumference of the sea urchins, discarding the mouth area. Use a small spoon to remove the edible part – that is the orange-colour-ed star-shaped section – and put into a dish Prepare the tomato sauce separately in a pan. Start by gently sautéing the finely chopped garlic, onion, and parsley, and as soon as the onion begins to soften add the peeled tomatoes, a small piece of chilli pepper and salt. Leave to cook slowly, adding a little warm water and a little fish stock if necessary.
When the sauce begins to thicken, add the sea urchin flesh and cook for around another 10 minutes. Cook the linguine in boiling salted water. Drain before they are completely cooked, and then toss them in the frying-pan with the sea urchin sauce.

The meat of the sea urchin (Paracentrotus lividus) *has a very rich and intense taste. In fact, the part of the sea urchin eaten is the roe, or rather the gonads. As a result, only the females – which are easy to identify by their purplish colour – are used for food.*

29.
Maccheroni dell'Alta Maremma - *Maremma Tagliatelle*
Grosseto

Ingredients:

500 g fresh egg pasta (tagliatelle)
1 sausage
50 g pancetta (or green bacon)
15 g dried porcini mushrooms
150 g chicken liver
100 g rabbit liver
3 walnuts
300 g peeled tomatoes
onion, carrot, celery stalk and parsley
red wine
grated Parmesan cheese
olive oil
1 pinch chilli pepper
salt

Steep the dried mushrooms in water. Clean and chop the liver. Chop the onion, carrot, celery and parsley finely. Tip into a pan and sweat gently in a little olive oil. Add the crumbled sausage and the finely chopped pancetta and walnuts. Sauté all together and pour over half a glass of red wine. Season with salt and a pinch of chilli pepper then add the mushrooms, drained and cut into small pieces. Cook for a few minutes and then add the chopped peeled tomatoes. Continue cooking over a low heat for around 30 minutes, then add the liver and cook for a further 10 minutes. Cook the tagliatelle in boiling salted water, then drain and tip into a bowl. Pour over the sauce, and complete with grated Parmesan cheese.

30.

Maccheroni alla pistoiese con sugo di carne
Pistoia Pasta with Meat Sauce
Pistoia

Ingredients:

> 500 g fresh egg pasta (maltagliati)
> 1 medium onion
> 1 celery stalk
> 1 carrot
> 400 g minced beef
> 250 g tomato sauce
> ½ glass red wine
> rosemary
> olive oil
> salt and pepper

Chop the onion, carrot and celery finely and sauté gently in four tablespoons of oil over a medium heat. Tip in the minced beef and continue cooking, add half a glass of red wine and let it evaporate. Then add the tomato sauce, season with salt and pepper and add two or three sprigs of rosemary. As soon as it begins to boil, lower the heat and leave to cook for two hours, adding a little stock if required.

Cook the pasta in plenty of boiling salted water, drain well and combine with the sauce.

31.

Maccheroni sull'ocio - *Pasta in Duck Sauce*
Arezzo

Ingredients:

600 g fresh egg pasta cut into large squares of about 10 cm
half a white goose
100 g Tuscan cured ham
onion, carrot and celery
300 g peeled tomatoes
meat stock
nutmeg
grated Parmesan cheese
breadcrumbs
olive oil
salt and pepper

Cut the goose into pieces, setting the liver aside, and put it in a casserole with four tablespoons of oil, the chopped carrot, onion and celery and the chopped ham. Season with salt and pepper and a little nutmeg. Sauté over a lively heat for around ten minutes. Add the tomatoes and continue cooking, ladling over a little stock from time to time. After around 45 minutes add the chopped goose liver and continue cooking for another 15 minutes. Cook the pasta in plenty of boiling salted water for a few minutes. Drain and place the pasta squares in a buttered baking dish, spooning the goose sauce over each layer as for lasagne, and sprinkling each layer with the grated Parmesan. Make the last layer with sauce and Parmesan mixed with breadcrumbs.
Place in a pre-heated oven for five minutes. Serve the pasta and the pieces of goose separately.

This dish used to be prepared towards the end of June to celebrate the festival that was held on the farm at the time when the wheat was threshed. In the Arezzo dialect 'ocio' is the name used for the 'oca', or goose.

32.
Maltagliati al cinghiale - *Maltagliati in Wild Boar Sauce*
Lucca / Grosseto / Massa Carrara

Ingredients:

500 g fresh egg pasta (maltagliati)
600 g lean wild boar meat
100 g white onions
100 g celery (stalks only)
100 g carrots
½ litre tomato sauce
1 tablespoon tomato concentrate
1 hot chilli pepper
200 ml meat stock
olive oil
300 ml red wine
2 cloves garlic
salt
black pepper

Marinate the wild boar meat in the red wine, with garlic, onion, celery and bay leaves for at least 12 hours.

When the time is up, clean and chop the onions and the garlic and sauté gently in olive oil in a large saucepan. Add the finely chopped celery and carrot and cook everything gently.

After 5-10 minutes, add the wild boar meat – drained and cut very fine with a knife or passed through the mincer. Sauté this too and then season with salt, add the meat stock and, last of all, the red wine.

When the wine has completely evaporated, add the tomato concentrate and the tomato sauce. Leave to cook over a slow heat, stirring every so often, until the sauce has thickened. Continue cooking until the meat is thoroughly tender, adding hot water if necessary.

Cook the pasta in plenty of boiling salted water, drain, and serve with the wild boar sauce.
A sprinkle of grated lemon zest can be used to enhance the aroma.

Casertana o Pelatella.

Yorkshire.

Limosina.

Piemontese, *detta di Cavour*.

Anglo-cinese.

Hampshire.

Derived from *Sus scrofa* and *palustris*, over the centuries the pig has given rise to a multiplicity of micro-breeds at local level.

33.
Panzanella – *Tomato and Bread Salad*
Florence / Prato / Massa Carrara / Lucca / Livorno

Ingredients for 6:

> 500 g stale Tuscan bread
> 3 ripe tomatoes
> 2 red onions
> basil
> red wine vinegar
> olive oil
> salt

Slice the bread and leave it to soak in cold water for 15 minutes, then squeeze it out, break into small pieces and tip into a bowl.
Add the tomatoes chopped into chunks, the finely sliced onions and a few leaves of basil.
Garnish with plenty of olive oil, salt and vinegar and mix gently.
Set aside to rest and when you are ready to serve, add another trickle of oil and a teaspoon of vinegar.

In some parts of Tuscany, in addition to the above ingredients, chicory, fennel, anchovies, tuna, hard-boiled eggs and so on may also be added.

34.

Pappardelle all'aretina - *Arezzo Pappardelle*
Arezzo

Ingredients:

500 g fresh egg pasta (pappardelle)
1 duck (approx. 1 kilo in weight)
100 g cured ham
1 onion
1 celery stalk
1 carrot
sage
basil
300 g peeled tomatoes
1 glass dry white wine
grated Parmesan cheese (or Grana Padana)
butter
salt and pepper
olive oil

Clean the duck, setting the liver aside, and cut it into small pieces.
Heat two tablespoons of oil in a pan and gently sweat the chopped vegetables and the chopped ham. Stir well, then add the duck meat. Let the flavours blend for a while, then pour in the white wine and let it evaporate. Add the tomatoes, season with salt and pepper and leave to cook for about one and a half hours.
Ten minutes before cooking time is up, add the chopped liver. Remove the pieces of duck meat from the pan and keep warm. Sieve the sauce.
Cook the pasta in plenty of boiling salted water, drain, and pour the duck sauce over it, mix it in adding a knob of butter. Sprinkle with the grated cheese and serve.
The pieces of duck can be served separately.

35.

Penne del cacciatore - *Hunter's Pasta*
Pisa / Siena

Ingredients:

350 g pasta (penne lisce)
150 g pheasant meat
150 g peeled tomatoes
40 g pancetta (or green bacon)
onion, carrot and celery stalk
sage
3 juniper berries
red wine
vegetable stock
olive oil
salt
black pepper

Finely chop the vegetables, the pancetta and the sage and sweat gently in a little olive oil.

Add the chopped pheasant meat and season with salt. When the meat is well-coloured, pour over half a glass of red wine and let it evaporate.

Add the tomatoes and cook for at least one hour, adding a little vegetable stock from time to time.

When the time is up, add the juniper berries and cook for a few more minutes, then remove the pieces of pheasant.

Cook the pasta in plenty of boiling salted water and drain before it is completely cooked, then toss it in the pan with the sauce.

Serve the pasta with the pieces of pheasant on the top.

36.
Penne strascicate – *Pan-Tossed Pasta with Meat Sauce*
Prato / Florence

Ingredients:

350 g pasta (penne rigate)
olive oil
grated Parmesan cheese
350 g leftover roast meat
1 carrot
1 onion
1 celery stalk
1 bay leaf
1 tin peeled tomatoes
dry white wine
meat stock
salt

Chop the onion, carrot and celery stalk finely and sauté gently over a slow heat in four tablespoons of oil in a large pot without a lid.

When the vegetables are nice and soft, add the finely chopped leftover meat and pour in half a glass of white wine. When the wine has evaporated, add the peeled tomatoes and the bay leaf. Cook over a slow heat with the lid on for about twenty minutes. Adjust salt to taste and, if necessary, add a little meat stock. Cook the pasta in boiling salted water and drain a good while before it is completely cooked, taking care to keep about a cupful of the cooking water. Put five or six tablespoons of the meat sauce into a large pan along with a couple of tablespoons of oil and add the pasta. Sprinkle with plenty of grated Parmesan and continue cooking, gradually adding ladlefuls of the pasta cooking water, stirring thoroughly all the time.

Remove from the heat while the pasta is still firm, and serve immediately, with more grated cheese if you wish.

37.

Pennette al sugo di selvaggina - *Pasta in Game Sauce*

Lucca

Ingredients:

350 g pasta (pennette)
100 g hare meat
100 g minced beef
100 g rabbit meat
stock
onion, carrot and celery stalk
1 glass red wine
olive oil
salt and pepper
rosemary

Sweat the finely chopped carrot, onion and celery in a large pot in three tablespoons of oil. Add the roughly chopped hare and rabbit meat and the minced beef and sauté.

Then add a glass of red wine and let it evaporate, season with salt and pepper and moisten with stock.

Cook over a low heat for around an hour, adding more stock as necessary. Cook the pasta and serve with the game sauce, garnishing with a couple of sprigs of rosemary.

38.
Pici al sugo di carne - *Pici in Meat Sauce*
Siena / Grosseto

Ingredients:

500 g fresh pici
150 g minced beef
150 g minced pork
1 sausage
300 g tomato sauce
1 carrot
1 celery stalk
1 onion
2 cloves garlic
a little parsley
olive oil
½ glass red wine
salt

Chop all the vegetables and the parsley by hand on a chopping board, then tip into a deep pot (preferably earthenware) with three tablespoons of oil. Sauté gently over a moderate heat. Add the two types of mince and the sausage mashed with a fork, and continue cooking, stirring all the time.

When the meat is evenly browned, turn up the heat, pour in the wine and add the tomato sauce. Season with salt and put the lid on the pot, then cook over a very low heat for about an hour.

If you like, you can add fresh mushrooms, or dried porcini that have been steeped in water and drained.

Cook the pasta in plenty of boiling salted water, drain and mix in the sauce.

Pici are thick, hand-rolled spaghetti-type pasta made using soft wheat flour, oil and salt, to be used without delay as soon as they are prepared.

Dry pici are instead made with durum wheat flour, bear no comparison to the fresh version and also require longer cooking.

Pici go perfectly with meat or game sauces, but also with mushrooms and other types of condiment. .

39.
Pici all'aglione – *Pici in Garlic Sauce*
Siena / Grosseto

Ingredients:

500 g fresh pici
250 g peeled tomatoes
8 large cloves garlic
1 pinch chilli pepper
olive oil
salt

Cut the garlic cloves into large pieces and sauté them gently in a saucepan with four tablespoons of oil and a pinch of chilli pepper (optional).
After a few minutes, add the peeled tomatoes chopped into small pieces and cook for around 15 minutes. Season with salt to taste.
In the meantime, cook the pici in plenty of boiling salted water.
Drain the pasta and mix into the garlic sauce. Serve piping hot.

This dish is generally made using 'aglione': a type of garlic that is grown in particular in the Valdichiana. Aglione belongs to the same family as ordinary garlic and the colour is the same but the cloves are much larger and can weigh up to 80 grams each.

40.
Pici sulle briciole – *Pici in Breadcrumbs*
Siena / Grosseto

Ingredients:

> 500 g fresh pici
> 4 slices of stale Tuscan bread (around 60 g in all)
> olive oil
> grated mature Pecorino cheese
> 2 cloves garlic
> salt
> dry chilli pepper

Break the bread into large crumbs. Sweat the garlic in a pan with four tablespoons of oil, add the bread and sauté until golden with a pinch of chilli pepper.

In the meantime, cook the pici in plenty of boiling salted water. Drain, then tip into the pan and toss them well in the sauce.

Serve with lashings of grated Pecorino cheese.

41.
Polenta con sugo di funghi – *Polenta with Mushroom Sauce*
Lucca

Ingredients for 6:

> 700 g cooked polenta (cornmeal)
> 500 g minced beef
> 2 sausages
> 15 g dried porcini mushrooms
> 250 g peeled tomatoes
> 1 onion
> 1 celery stalk
> 1 carrot
> stock
> ½ glass red wine
> olive oil
> salt and pepper

Steep the dried mushrooms in a cup of cold water.
Chop the onion, carrot and celery finely and sauté in three tablespoons of oil.
Add the minced beef and the crumbled sausages and brown, stirring all the time.
Pour in the red wine and let it evaporate, then add the drained mushrooms.
Add the peeled tomatoes, season with salt and pepper and cook for around 40 minutes, adding stock from time to time if required.
Serve the polenta with the sauce spooned over it.

Polenta is made by sprinkling the cornmeal into a pot of boiling salted water and mixing continuously until it is cooked. Otherwise, you can also use instant polenta, following the cooking times on the packet, or even loaves of ready-made polenta.

42.
Minestra di pane - *Bread Soup*
Florence

Ingredients:

300 g stale Tuscan bread
400 g dried cannellini beans
1 head Tuscan kale
½ small Savoy cabbage
3 bunches chard
1 potato
1 carrot
1 celery stalk
2 onions
1 tablespoon tomato conserve
olive oil
salt and pepper

Boil the beans, starting in cold water, then purée about three-quarters and tip the puree back into the cooking water.

In another large pot, sauté one chopped onion in five tablespoons of oil. As soon as it begins to soften, add the tomato conserve diluted with the bean water. Slice the other onion, slice the carrot and the celery, chop the chard and the two cabbages into thin strips and peel and slice the potato. Tip all the vegetables into the pot with the onion.

Season with salt and pepper and cook with the lid on for five minutes, then pour in all the bean water. Cook for about one hour, then add the whole beans. Switch off the heat, stir well and leave to cool slightly. Ladle into a large tureen, interspersing with layers of thinly sliced bread.

Leave to sit for a few hours.

Any soup that is left over can be used the following day to make the famous *ribollita*.

43.
Ribollita - *Reheated Vegetable and Bean Soup*
Florence

To make ribollita, leave the bread soup to sit for 24 hours, then reheat it in a pot, preferably earthenware, and bring it to the boil again, adding olive oil. Serve with another drizzle of olive oil and perhaps – to notch up the rudeness index – with finely-sliced fresh onion.

La Grasse Cuisine, engraving by Pieter Brueghel the Elder, 1563.

44.
Spaghetti sul favollo – *Spaghetti with Crab*
Livorno

Ingredients:

350 g spaghetti
500 g warty crabs
250 g peeled tomatoes
1 tablespoon tomato concentrate
½ glass olive oil
½ glass white wine
2 cloves garlic
half a chilli pepper
sage
salt

Place the oil and the sage in a large pan. Sauté with the finely chopped garlic and chilli pepper. Remove the sage, add the crabs in large chunks and continue sautéing over a high heat.
Pour in the wine and let it evaporate. Then add the tomatoes, mashed with a fork, and the tomato concentrate diluted in a little hot water.
Season with salt, put on the lid and cook over a slow heat for about twenty minutes.
In the meantime, cook the spaghetti, draining them before they are completely cooked, then tip them into the crab sauce and mix thoroughly over a lively heat.
Serve the spaghetti piping hot.

The warty crab (Eriphia verrucosa) *is definitely the most flavoursome and rudest of all the crabs. It is a shallow water crab, found in the Black Sea, Mediterranean Sea and the eastern Atlantic Ocean. It is easily recognisable by its dark red colour, and can grow up to a size of 9 cm in width.*

45.
Stracci sul papero – *Gander Tagliatelle*
Prato

ngredients (for 6):

700 g fresh egg pasta (tagliatelle or stracci)
1 gander of around 2 kg, already cleaned
300 g minced beef
1 carrot
1 celery stalk
1 onion
1 bunch of rosemary and sage tied together
1 glass red wine
600 g peeled tomatoes
½ glass tomato conserve
olive oil
1 teaspoon fennel flowers
salt

Chop the cleaned duck into pieces.
In a large saucepan gently sweat the chopped carrot, celery and onion and the bunch of sage and rosemary. When the vegetables are nicely softened add the chunks of duck and the minced beef. Sauté until the meat is well browned, then pour in the wine and let it evaporate and season with salt.
Add the tomatoes and the tomato conserve, adjust salt to taste and add the fennel flowers. Cook with the lid on for 2 hours.
Cook the tagliatelle in boiling salted water for a few minutes, drain and mix into the duck sauce.
Serve the pieces of duck as a second course or as an accompaniment to the pasta.

46.
Tordelli lucchesi - *Lucca Tordelli*
Lucca

Ingredients:

For the pasta:
    400 g plain or all-purpose flour
    4 eggs
    1 tablespoon olive oil

For the filling:
    50 g lean beef
    150 g lean pork
    50 g Mortadella sausage
    50 g Tuscan cured ham
    2 eggs
    2 slices of stale Tuscan bread soaked in meat stock
    50 g grated Parmesan cheese
    60 g extra virgin olive oil
    ½ onion,
    ½ carrot
    1 celery stalk
    1 clove garlic
    1 sprig parsley
    nutmeg
    leaves of wild thyme (*Thymus serpyllum*)
    salt and pepper

For the sauce:
    500 g meat sauce (already prepared)

Pour the flour onto a board in a heap, then make a hollow in the centre and break in the two eggs along with a tablespoon of extra virgin olive oil. Knead thoroughly, working until you have smooth ball of paste and then set it aside to rest in a covered bowl.

Place the slices of Tuscan bread to steep in a bowl of meat stock.

Clean and chop the garlic, onion, celery and carrot and tip into a saucepan with olive oil. Sauté until they turn soft, then add the meat chopped into chunks and the parsley and thyme and complete the cooking.

Pass through a mincer the meat and vegetable sauce and the cooking juices along with the soaked bread, the ham and the Mortadella. Tip into a large bowl and add the eggs, the grated Parmesan cheese and a pinch of grated nutmeg. Mix thoroughly and adjust salt to taste.

Roll out the pasta into strips of about 3 fingers in width. Spoon a little of the filling onto the strips at regular intervals. Fold the pasta over and cut out using the special mould or the rim of a glass. Continue until all the ingredients are used up.

Cook the tordelli in plenty of boiling salted water, letting them boil for just a few minutes. Remove with a slotted spoon, drain well, and place them in layers in a tureen, spooning the prepared meat sauce over each layer.

Serve immediately, piping hot, adding a sprinkle of grated Parmesan cheese on each plate.

47.
Zuppa alla volterrana – *Volterra Soup*
Pisa / Siena

Ingredients for 6:

1 onion
2 carrots
½ kg potatoes
1 celery stalk
basil
thyme and lesser calamint (*Clinopodium nepeta*)
½ glass olive oil
300 g boiled fresh cannellini beans
5-6 leaves Tuscan kale
2 very ripe tomatoes
1½ litres stock or warm water
a few slices of lightly toasted Tuscan bread

Chop the onion, carrot, celery and basil finely and sauté gently in a saucepan with half a glass of oil and a pinch of salt and pepper. When the vegetables begin to turn golden and soft, add the peeled potatoes chopped into chunks. As soon as the potatoes begin to brown, add the boiled beans and the chopped leaves of Tuscan kale.
Cook for a few minutes, then add two very ripe tomatoes that you have already tossed in a little oil and seasoned with just a little salt and pepper.
Leave to cook for a few more minutes then pour in about one and a half litres of stock or warm water, the thyme and the lesser calamint. Bring to the boil, then leave to simmer for at least an hour.
Serve with slices of lightly toasted Tuscan bread.

SECOND COURSES

Previous page: a satirical vignette by Giuseppe Novello, from *Il signore di buona famiglia* (Mondadori 1942). 'When no change of crockery is scheduled . . . and the guest leaves his cutlery on the plate.'

48.
Anguille agli aromi - *Eels in Tomato and Herb Sauce*
Lucca

Ingredients:

1 kg eels
400 g ripe tomatoes
celery
parsley
rosemary
sage
1 carrot
garlic
1 glass white wine
flour
olive oil
salt
1 pinch chilli pepper

Clean, gut and peel the eels then chop them into pieces of five or six centimetres.
Wash, dry and coat in flour. Finely chop the garlic, celery, parsley, carrot, rosemary and sage and sauté in a large pan in three tablespoons of olive oil. Toss in the pieces of floured eel and cook until golden, then pour in the white wine and let it evaporate.
Peel the tomatoes and chop them into pieces then add to the pan. Season with salt and add a pinch of chilli pepper.
Cook for around twenty minutes.

The European eel (Anguilla anguilla) *lives in freshwater, but returns to the ocean to spawn and to die. After 5–20 years in fresh or brackish water, the eels become sexually mature, and they begin their migration back to the sea to spawn.*

49.

Baccalà ricco alla livornese – *Livorno Salt Cod*
Pisa / Livorno

Ingredients:

800 g salt cod, steeped in water
400 g ripe tomatoes
1 large white onion
2 cloves garlic
flour
olive oil
parsley
salt and pepper

Dry the salt cod, remove the skin, cut into chunks and coat in flour.
In a large pan, heat plenty of oil with the garlic cloves and fry the pieces of cod for 5 minutes on each side until they are golden. Leave to dry on absorbent kitchen paper.
Slice the onion finely and sweat it gently in a large pan with three tablespoons of oil. When the onion becomes transparent, add the peeled, deseeded and diced tomatoes. Stir well and season with salt and pepper. Cook for around 15 minutes, then lay the pieces of fried cod in the pan and continue cooking for another 10 minutes.
Serve, sprinkled if you like with fresh chopped parsley.

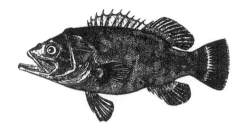

50.
Cacciucco all'elbana - *Elba Fish Soup*
Livorno

Ingredients for 6:

For the fish stock
500 g rockfish
olive oil
1 medium-size onion
1 carrot
1 celery stalk
1 glass dry white wine
2 bay leaves
salt and chilli pepper

For the soup:
300 g cuttlefish
500 g octopus
1 kg soup fish (common smooth-hound, gurnard, red gurnard, European, moray eel, weever, red scorpionfish, locust lobster, mussels, or similar, as available)
12 crabs
1 onion
6 cloves garlic
3-4 sage leaves
1 glass dry white wine
½ glass tomato conserve
handful of chopped parsley
chilli pepper
olive oil - salt

To prepare the fish stock, place a large pot on the heat with the chopped carrot, onion and celery and a good slosh of oil. Sauté well, adding the rockfish and all the discarded pieces of the fish for the soup. Add the white wine and let it evaporate, then add enough cold water to completely cover everything. Season with salt, chilli pepper and bay leaves and leave to simmer for at least half an hour. When the time is up, push the rockfish through a food mill, then tip it back into the stock and leave it to cool for a little.

To prepare the fish soup: chop the cuttlefish and octopus into big chunks and the other fish into small slices or pieces. Finely chop the onion, garlic, sage and chilli pepper and sweat it in oil in a large saucepan.

Add the cuttlefish, octopus and shellfish and sauté for a few minutes until the octopus turns a nice violet colour. Pour over the white wine and let it evaporate, then add the tomato conserve (this is preferable to fresh tomato because it does not sweeten the soup as much). Leave to cook for about a quarter of an hour, moistening with a ladleful of the fish stock from time to time and gradually adding the remaining fish, based on the cooking times. Leave to simmer over a moderate heat, continuing to moisten with the fish stock. Add the mussels just before the soup is completely cooked. Adjust the seasoning, bearing in mind that it should be quite spicy.

Serve with slices of toasted bread lightly rubbed with garlic and a sprinkle of fresh chopped parsley.

Legend has it that cacciucco is a fish soup that was invented by the fishermen using the unsold remains of the previous day's catch. Obviously, it was mostly made up of cheap fish that varied in quantity and type depending on the season and the abundance or scarcity of fish at the time. This is the most famous recipe, the Livorno version, which is not very different from that of Elba. In Livorno they say that to make cacciucco you need to have at least five different types of fish, one for each of the 'c's in the name of the dish. The Elba version of cacciucco is less elaborate, since the conger, the moray eel and the weever are left out. Far from being a simple fish soup, cacciucco is actually quite complex to prepare. For instance, the cuttlefish and the octopus have to be cooked separately and the mussels have to be added at the very last minute, since there's nothing worse than soggy, overcooked mussels.

Although cacciucco contains many different varieties of fish, they all come magically together in an amalgam of flavours and fragrances that conjure up a deliciously appetising savour of the sea.

51.
Capretto alla cacciatora - *Kid or Lamb Cacciatore*
Massa Carrara

Ingredients for 6:

1 kg goat meat (kid)
100 g lardo
3 tablespoons olive oil
1 glass white wine
3 medium-sized tomatoes
1 clove garlic
1 sprig of rosemary
salt and pepper

Finely chop the lardo, rosemary and garlic and sauté in a pot with oil.
Add the goat meat cut into fairly large pieces and brown over a moderate heat, stirring all the time.
Pour over the white wine and let it evaporate gently.
Peel and seed the tomatoes and remove any water then chop into small pieces and toss into the pot.
Cook for around one and a half hours, adding hot water from time to time if necessary.
Season with salt and pepper shortly before removing from the heat.

For this recipe we recommend using the meat of a young kid of not more than 8 kilos. Lamb can also be used instead of kid.

52.

Capriolo al sapore di bosco – *Forest Flavour Venison*
Lucca / Pisa / Massa Carrara

Ingredients:

800 g venison
1 litre red wine
mixed vegetables and herbs (for marinade)
100 g pancetta (or green bacon)
1 onion
1 carrot
bay leaves
juniper berries
rosemary
stock
olive oil
salt and pepper

Chop the venison into pieces and marinate in a bowl for twelve hours in a litre of red wine with vegetables and aromatic herbs of your choice.
Filter the wine of the marinade and keep to one side.
Chop the carrot, onion, rosemary and pancetta and sauté in a large saucepan with four tablespoons of olive oil. When the onion has softened, add the drained and dried venison along with a few bay leaves, a teaspoon of juniper berries, salt and pepper.
Continue to sauté for about 15 minutes, then pour in half of the wine from the marinade.
Let the sauce reduce slowing, turning the meat regularly.
Complete cooking, moistening every so often with more wine from the marinade.
Serve hot with boiled potatoes or peas.

53.
Cervello alla fiorentina - *Fried Calf Brains*
Florence

Ingredients for 6:

800 g calf's brains
½ onion
2 eggs
breadcrumbs
flour
3 lemons
chopped parsley
olive oil
oil for frying
salt and pepper

Blanch the brains in boiling salted water for around 3 minutes and then peel off the membrane.

Place in a bowl of cold water with the juice of one lemon for around one hour. Cut the brains into slices of about one centimetre and place them in a marinade made of oil, chopped parsley, sliced onion, salt and pepper for about 2 hours. Coat the slices in flour and then dip into the beaten eggs and then in the breadcrumbs.

Fry in hot oil and serve accompanied by slices of lemon.

54.
Chiocciole alla stiglianese – *Stigliano Snails*
Siena

Ingredients:

80 medium-sized purged snails
2 thin slices of salami
1 slice Finocchiona
1 slice Soprassata
2 thin slices of Mortadella sausage
300 g peeled tomatoes
1 clove garlic
1 onion
1 glass red wine
stock
Tuscan bread
olive oil
salt and pepper

Chop the garlic and onion and tip into a large pot with three tablespoons of oil.
Then add the finely chopped sausages and salami. Sauté for a few minutes then add the purged snails.
Pour in a glass of red wine and a cup of hot stock. Cook for around half an hour, then add the tomatoes, season with salt and pepper and continue cooking for another two hours. Add a little more hot stock from time to time if necessary.
Serve the snails in their sauce on slices of toasted Tuscan bread.

The snails have to go through a lengthy purging process using water and aromatic herbs before cooking. If you want to save yourself this extra work, you can buy them ready-purged from the fishmonger or at the supermarket.

55.
Chiocciole alla moda di Camaiore – *Camaiore Snails*
Lucca

Ingredients:

80 medium-sized snails
200 g tomato sauce
1 clove garlic
sage
1 glass white wine
vinegar
olive oil
salt and pepper

Blanch the snails in boiling salted water for five minutes then wash them in water and vinegar.
Chop the garlic and sage finely and sauté in a large pot in three tablespoons of oil. Tip in the snails and pour over a glass of white wine. When the wine has evaporated add the tomato sauce.
Season with salt and pepper and cook over a low heat with the lid on for around two hours, adding a little hot water from time to time.

56.
Cibrèo – *Chicken Giblet Fricassée*
Florence

Ingredients:

12 chicken livers
12 combs and wattles
24 chicken testicles
8 chicken hearts
1 egg yolk
1 onion
1 lemon
sage
nutmeg
white wine
stock
olive oil – salt and pepper

Blanch the combs, remove the skin and cut into slices. Finely chop the onion and sage and sauté in a saucepan in three tablespoons of oil, then add the combs and wattles coated in flour. After a couple of minutes pour over half a glass of white wine. Add the livers, the testicles and the hearts chopped into pieces. Add a pinch of nutmeg, season with salt and pepper and continue cooking for around twenty minutes, adding a little hot stock as required. When cooking is complete, add the egg yolk beaten with the juice of half a lemon. Stir for a few seconds and serve piping hot.

The origin of the word 'cibrèo' is unknown. Some believe that it could derive from the Arabic term 'zingiberensi' which means 'dish of the king made with ginger'. Others say it derives from the old French 'civé, meaning sauce, from 'cive', onion, which in turn originates from the Latin 'cepa'. Despite the decidedly 'rude' ingredients, Pellegrino Artusi in his famous cookbook defined it as 'a simple, fine, and delicate dish, suitable for ladies with languishing appetites and convalescents.'

57.
Cioncia - *Valdinievole Calf's Head Stew*
Pistoia / Lucca

Ingredients:

600 g calf's head
1 onion
1 clove garlic
300 g peeled tomatoes
lesser calamint (*Clinopodium nepeta*)
½ glass red wine
Tuscan bread
olive oil
salt and pepper

Boil all the parts of the calf's head (ears, lips, cheeks etc.) in plenty of boiling salted water for at least an hour. Leave to cool and then cut into strips.
Chop the onion and garlic finely and sauté in a large pot with four tablespoons of oil; as soon as they are softened, add the meat.
Continue cooking for fifteen minutes, then pour in half a glass of red wine and let it evaporate. Add the peeled tomatoes and continue cooking for another hour, adding hot stock as required.
Serve the stew on slices of toasted Tuscan bread.

'Cioncia' is an ancient and distinctly rude dish of the Valdinievole. It appears to have been invented by the workers who transported the animal hides to be tanned, a process known in Italian as 'concia'. It was traditionally made using the offcuts of flesh still clinging to the hides, in particular the nose, ears and lips.

58.
Collo ripieno - *Stuffed Chicken Neck*
Lucca / Arezzo / Pisa / Florence

Ingredients:

2 boned and cleaned chicken necks
200 g minced beef
200 g minced pork
3 eggs
bunch of mixed herbs
70 g grated Parmesan cheese
breadcrumbs
nutmeg
olive oil
salt and pepper

Sauté the minced meats in a saucepan in four tablespoons of oil. Leave to cool, and then pass through the mincer to get a smooth texture.
Add three tablespoons of breadcrumbs, the eggs and a little grated nutmeg, and season with salt and pepper.
Use this paste to stuff the chicken necks then tie them up with string and boil slowly in salted water with the bunch of herbs for about 45 minutes.
Leave them to cool in the cooking water then cut into slices.
Serve with mixed pickles or a homemade mayonnaise.

It is increasingly rare to find this dish in even the most traditional trattorias. In addition to the above ingredients, you can also add a little grated lemon zest.

59.
Coratella fritta - *Fried Offal*
Pistoia / Prato / Florence

Ingredients:

600 g lamb offal (liver, lung, heart and spleen)
flour
corn oil for frying
lemon
salt

The 'scorticagnelli', or lamb skinner, in a seventeenth-century engraving, copy of print from the *Arti di Bologna* by Annibale Carracci (1560-1609)

Chop the liver, lung, spleen and heart into small chunks, coat in flour and fry in plenty of hot oil.
Serve sprinkled with salt and a few drops of lemon juice.

The term 'coratella' refers to the windpipe and other connected parts such as the lungs, heart and liver. It can also be cooked in sauce, or plain with sage and rosemary. In Maremma they also make a tasty dish using wild boar offal in tomato sauce. .

60.
Fegatelli della fattoria – *Farmhouse Faggots*
Arezzo / Pisa / Lucca

Ingredients:

400 g pig's liver
200 g pig's caul fat (omentum membrane)
white breadcrumbs, lightly toasted
wild fennel seeds
oil
salt
pepper

Cut the caul fat into 12 large squares and put them to steep in a large bowl full of warm water.
Divide the liver into 12 cubes of 3 cm.
In a small bowl mix the breadcrumbs with a pinch of salt, a pinch of pepper and half a tablespoon of fennel seeds. Roll the liver chunks in this mixture to coat them then wrap each one in a square of the drained and squeezed caul fat, securing it with a toothpick.
Place the liver faggots in a pan brushed with oil and cook them rapidly over a moderate heat for 8 minutes.
Alternatively, you can spear the faggots onto skewers, alternated with chunks of bread and cubes of pancetta (or green bacon) and cook them in a moderate oven for 15 minutes brushing them with oil a couple of times.
Serve hot.

Liver prepared in this way can be conserved in glass jars covered with melted lard.
This recipe is quite similar to that of British faggots, traditionally made from offal,
usually pork, and other rude animal parts that are generally discarded. Nowadays, just
liver tends to be used, again wrapped in either caul fat or bacon.

61.

Francesina – *Leftover Boiled Meat Stew*
Florence / Pisa / Livorno / Siena

Ingredients:

600 g leftover boiled meat
4 red onions (preferably from Certaldo)
1 flat tablespoon of tomato concentrate
meat stock
olive oil
salt and pepper

Clean the onions, chop into thin slices and soften them in a pot covered with a little water for about half an hour, taking care that they don't stick. When they're nice and soft, add a little olive oil, a tablespoon of tomato concentrate, meat stock and the boiled meat cut into slices. Season with salt and pepper.
Cook for another half hour, or until the sauce is well thickened.
Serve piping hot.

The recipe for Francesina varies depending on the part of Tuscany it comes from. In Prato it is known as 'Stiracchio', whereas in the province of Lucca it is made using eggs.

62.
Frittata col lesso rifatto – *Leftover Boiled Meat Omelette*
Pistoia / Prato / Florence

Ingredients:

6 eggs
200 g leftover boiled meat
1 onion
125 g peeled tomatoes
olive oil
salt and pepper

Chop the onion into thin slices and sauté in two tablespoons of oil in a large frying pan.
Add the boiled meat cut into chunks and the peeled tomatoes. Season with salt and pepper and cook for fifteen minutes
Beat the eggs with a pinch of salt and pour in with the meat. Put the lid on the pan and cook until the egg has set.

To turn over the omelette, place a large plate over the frying pan and turn quickly over so that the omelette falls onto the plate, then slide it gently back into the pan to cook the other side.

63.
Fritto misto toscano – *Tuscan Mixed Fry*
Florence / Prato / Pistoia

Ingredients for 6:

8 lamb cutlets
4 slices of veal
500 g brains and sweetbreads
2 zucchini
4 artichokes
3 eggs
flour
4 slices of Tuscan bread
½ glass white wine
breadcrumbs
olive oil
salt
corn oil for frying

Blanch the brains and sweetbreads for a couple of minutes in boiling salted water. Then peel off the membranes and cut into slices. Coat in flour, then beat two eggs in a bowl and dip them in and season with salt.

Dip the lamb cutlets and the veal slices into the beaten egg too, then coat them in breadcrumbs.

In a bowl make a batter by beating one egg with three tablespoons of sifted flour, a tablespoon of olive oil, half a glass of white wine and a little salt. Tip in the sliced zucchini.

Cut the artichokes into wedges and coat them in flour.

Begin frying in plenty of hot oil, starting with the meat and then continuing with the vegetables. When you have finished, dip the slices of Tuscan bread into the batter and fry these too.

Arrange the mixed fry on a platter lined with absorbent paper and sprinkle with salt before serving.

64.
Fritto d'avanzi – *Leftover Roast Fritters*
Lucca / Arezzo / Massa Carrara

Ingredients:

> 500 g leftover roast meat
> 100 g Mortadella sausage
> ½ onion
> flour
> 250 cl milk
> 40 g butter
> 2 eggs
> 4 tablespoons grated Parmesan cheese
> nutmeg
> corn oil for frying
> salt and pepper

Finely chop the meat and the Mortadella and mix well together.

Sweat the finely chopped onion in a large pot with the butter, then add two tablespoons of flour and then the milk, stirring constantly with a wooden spoon until you have a bechamel sauce with onion.

Remove from the heat and add the meat, one egg, the grated Parmesan, a little nutmeg, salt and pepper. Mix together well.

Spread the paste in a baking tray in such a way that it's about 2 cm high, then leave to cool.

Cut the paste into small lozenge shapes and dip them in the beaten egg and then the breadcrumbs.

Fry in plenty of hot oil.

65.

Gurguglione - *Stewed Vegetables*

Livorno

Ingredients for 6:

1 large onion
green, yellow and red peppers
4 large aubergines
4 zucchini
basil
parsley
600 g ripe tomatoes
olive oil
salt

The key to the success of this recipe is to have fresh vegetables.

Remove the stems of the peppers and cut into pieces. Chop the aubergines and zucchini into fairly large chunks, and roughly chop the tomatoes.

Cut the onion into thin slices.

Tip all the vegetables into a large pan with a glass of oil, a pinch of salt and the finely chopped basil and parsley.

Put on the lid and cook first at a lively heat and then turn down to moderate, keeping the lid on so that the vegetables cook in their liquid. Serve piping hot.

Similar vegetable recipes are found in various regions around the Mediterranean coast, for example 'ratatouille' in Provence and 'caponata' in Sicily.

66.
Involtini all'uovo della bisnonna Emma
Great Grandma Emma's Pork Rolls
Florence / Pistoia

Ingredients:

500 g sliced pork
1 egg
200 g bread crumb
½ glass milk
½ glass white wine
1 clove garlic
parsley
nutmeg
grated Grana cheese
olive oil
salt

Soak the bread crumb in half a glass of milk for about 15 minutes, then add the beaten egg, the finely chopped garlic and parsley, a pinch of nutmeg and two tablespoons of grated Grana cheese. Mix everything together and add salt to taste. Beat the pork slices to soften them and then dot them with a few flakes of butter and spread them with the paste. Roll them up and secure with a toothpick Put three tablespoons of extra virgin olive oil in a frying pan and brown the pork rolls on all sides, then pour over the wine and let it evaporate. Continue cooking for about ten minutes then remove from the heat.
Leave to cool, then cut into thick slices. Put them back in the pan and warm over a low heat for about five minutes.

This is a recipe of rustic origins and there are numerous variants, with different fillings being used depending on the area. Our grandmothers also used to make them in different ways and with different ingredients depending on the meat available.

67.
Lampredotto agli odori dell'orto
Classic Florentine Lampredotto
Florence

Ingredients:

600 g lampredotto, ready to cook
1 onion
1 carrot
1 celery stalk
parsley
4 ripe tomatoes
basil
garlic
olive oil
salt and pepper

Pour around 3 litres of water into a large pot, add the onion cut in half and the carrot and celery stalk in chunks, along with a bunch of parsley – and basil if in season.
Add salt and bring to the boil, then add the lampredotto and cook for around an hour.
Drain, and season the lampredotto simply with salt and pepper, or with a green sauce made with finely chopped parsley and garlic blended with good extra virgin olive oil.
Serve on a plate or, in the more classic 'street food' form, in a bread roll, split open and lightly moistened with the cooking juices.

Lampredotto is the darkest part of the tripe, consisting of the abomasum, or fourth stomach of ruminants.

68.
Lesso alla toscana – *Tuscan Boiled Meat*
Florence / Massa Carrara / Livorno

Ingredients for 6:

    900 g beef (shank, brisket, rump, etc.)
    half a hen, ready to cook
    1 onion
    1 carrot
    1 celery stalk
    salt

Pour three litres of water into a large saucepan. Add the roughly chopped carrot, onion and celery and the beef. Bring to the boil and put the lid on and cook for an hour and half.

When the time is up, add the half hen and continue cooking for another forty minutes.

Leave the meat to sit in its stock for an hour.

Serve by cutting the beef into slices and the hen into pieces, accompanied by green sauce or other sauce of your choice, or by homemade mayonnaise

In the past the boiled meat was eaten simply sprinkled with a little coarse sea salt.

69.
Lingua in umido – *Stewed Tongue*
Florence / Prato

Ingredients:

1 calf's tongue of about 700 g
300 g chopped peeled tomatoes
1 carrot
1 onion
1 celery stalk
1 lemon
1 bunch stock vegetables (carrot, celery, onion)
½ glass white wine
 stock
 60 g pancetta (or green bacon)
 olive oil
 salt and pepper

Boil the tongue in plenty of boiling salted water with the roughly chopped stock vegetables for around one and a half hours.

Leave to cool slightly, then peel the tongue and cut it into slices about one centimetre thick.

Finely chop the onion, carrot, celery and pancetta and sauté in a large pot in four tablespoons of olive oil. When the vegetables are softened add the slices of tongue and continue cooking for a few minutes. Pour over the white wine and let it evaporate, then add the tomatoes and season with salt and pepper.

Cook over a low heat with the lid on for about an hour, adding hot stock from time to time if required.

Serve the slices of tongue piping hot with a sprinkle of grated lemon zest.

70.
Magro in umido – *Stewed Lean Beef*
Florence

Ingredients:

1 kg beef (topside or silverside)
800 g tomato sauce
30 g butter
vegetable stock
1 onion
1 stalk celery
3 cloves garlic
olive oil
salt and pepper

Make a slit in the centre of the meat and slide in 3 cloves of garlic and the butter cut into small pieces and seasoned with salt and pepper.

In a saucepan, brown the meat in the oil on all sides, and then add the finely chopped onion and celery. Continue to sauté and then pour in a glass of red wine and let it evaporate. Add the tomato sauce and a little stock, and cook over a low heat for about an hour, adding more stock if required.

Once the meat is cooked leave it to cool, then cut into slices and put back into the pot with the sauce, which should be nice and thick.

Serve with a potato side dish of your choice, even mashed or creamed potatoes.

71.
Ossibuchi al limone - *Veal Shanks with Lemon*
Pistoia / Prato / Florence

Ingredients:

  4 cross-cut veal shanks (ossobuco)
  flour
  white wine
  1 unwaxed lemon
  rosemary
  1 clove garlic
  vegetable stock
  olive oil
  salt and pepper

Cut off the fat and the skin around the veal shanks.
Squash the whole garlic clove and sweat gently in a large pan with olive oil.
Coat the veal shanks in flour and pop them in the pan with a sprig of rosemary. Brown the shanks and then pour over half a glass of white wine and continue cooking until it has evaporated. Pour in half a litre of stock, season with salt and pepper and complete cooking. By the end, the cooking the juices should be thick and the meat tender.
Remove from the heat and garnish with grated lemon zest.

72.

Pancetta alla carrarina – *Stuffed Belly of Veal*

Massa Carrara

Ingredients for 6:

  1 kg veal belly
  200 g minced beef
  1 sausage
  300 g chard
  40 g grated Parmesan cheese
  100 g bread crumb
  milk
  2 eggs
  carrot, onion, celery stalk and parsley
  nutmeg
  olive oil
  salt and pepper

Prepare the filling with the minced beef, the crumbled sausage, the boiled and chopped chard, the bread crumb steeped in milk, the grated Parmesan cheese, the eggs, a sprinkle of grated nutmeg, salt and pepper.

Slit open the veal belly like a book (or you can ask the butcher to do this for you), then stuff it with the filling and roll it up. Stitch it and tie it so that it retains its shape and the filling stays inside.

Place in a pot of boiling water and continue to simmer for about one and a half hours. Leave it to cool in the water and then cut it into slices and serve, accompanied if you like by a sauce of your choice.

Veal belly is very rarely used nowadays since it is considered a cheap and poor-quality cut, and has sadly disappeared from many dishes. It is actually very flavoursome and, when well prepared, is very tasty even roasted.

73.
Pecora in umido - *Mutton Stew*
Florence / Prato

Ingredients for 6:

1 kg mutton
400 g peeled tomatoes
1 onion
1 carrot
1 celery stalk
1 clove garlic
red wine
olive oil
vinegar
salt and pepper

Cut the mutton into fairly large pieces, removing the fat and any sinews, then set to steep in cold water and vinegar for 12 hours.
Put the meat in a saucepan over a medium heat so that it can release its water along with any impurities.
Chop the garlic, onion, carrot and celery and sauté in a large saucepan with three tablespoons of olive oil. Add the pieces of mutton and brown them, then pour over a glass of red wine and let it evaporate. Add the tomatoes chopped into pieces and season with salt and pepper.
Cook for around two hours on a slow heat, adding a little hot water or stock from time to time if required. By the end, the meat should be absolutely tender.

Mutton is used mostly in the area of Campi Bisenzio and in the plain between Florence and Prato. Some recipes are also proposed in the Mugello area. In the old trattorias of Lunigiana you can also find a mutton stew made without tomato, more similar to the version common in England.

74.
Peposo imprunetino con patate
Impruneta Peposo Stew with Potatoes
Florence

Ingredients for 6:

1 kg beef shank
2 cloves garlic
½ litre Chianti red wine
rosemary
1 tablespoon black peppercorns
salt

Chop the meat into fairly large pieces and put it into a deep oven dish with the rosemary, garlic, black peppercorns, salt and wine. Add hot water to completely cover the meat.
Cover the oven dish and cook in a pre-heated oven at 140°C for about four hours, adding more water if necessary, until the meat is absolutely tender.
It can also be cooked on the hob over a very low heat in an earthenware pot, again for around four hours.
Serve with boiled potatoes.

75.

Piccioni in tegame con olive e salsiccia
Stuffed Pigeons with Olives
Siena

Ingredients:

4 pigeons, ready to cook
2 sausages
4 slices of lardo
200 g black olives
1 onion
2 cloves garlic
sage
white wine
stock
olive oil
salt and pepper

Stuff each pigeon with half a peeled sausage, then wrap a slice of lardo around the breast.

Tie up the pigeons so that they keep their shape during cooking. Place them in a casserole with four tablespoons of oil.

Peel and squash the garlic cloves and slice the onion and tip into the casserole with a few sage leaves.

Brown the pigeons on all sides for about ten minutes, then pour over a glass of white wine.

Season with salt and pepper and cook for about twenty minutes, moistening with a little stock from time to time and letting it evaporate slowly.

A few minutes before switching off the heat, untie the string and remove the lardo, then add the chopped pigeon livers and the stoned olives to the sauce.

Cook for another few minutes and serve piping hot.

76.

Pollo ruspante ripieno di castagne e prugne
Free-Range Chicken with Chestnut and Prune Stuffing
Lucca / Pisa

Ingredients for 6:

> 1 large free-range chicken
> 500 g chestnuts
> 3 sausages
> 200 g dried prunes
> 20 g dried Porcini mushrooms
> 2 eggs
> 1 apple
> bread crumb
> 50 g sliced pancetta (or green bacon)
> vin santo (or dessert wine)
> white wine
> olive oil – salt and pepper

Steep the prunes in a bowl of water, then drain. Do the same with the dried mushrooms. Boil the chestnuts then shell and peel them and chop them roughly. Peel and crumble the sausages and tip them into a bowl with the stoned and chopped prunes, the peeled and chopped apple and the chopped mushrooms. Mix thoroughly, then add a little bread crumb, the eggs, and a glass of vin santo. Season with salt and pepper and mix well until you have a smooth paste. Stuff the chicken and tie it up, wrapping the sliced pancetta round the breast. Put it in a baking dish with oil, white wine, salt and pepper, and place in a pre-heated oven at 180°C. Cook

for about one and a half hours, basting it frequently with the cooking juices. After one hour remove the pancetta so that the breast can brown nicely. The pancetta can then be served as an accompaniment.

77.
Polpette della zia Giulietta - *Auntie Giulietta's Meatballs*
Prato / Pistoia / Massa Carrara

Ingredients:

500 g minced beef
200 g minced pork
1 onion
3 tablespoons tomato sauce
2 eggs
2 egg yolks
grated Parmesan cheese
Tuscan bread
garlic
parsley
lemon zest
breadcrumbs
olive oil
salt and pepper

Lightly sauté the chopped onion in a saucepan in a little oil and then add the minced meat and brown it. Add the tomato sauce and half a glass of water, season with salt and pepper and cook for about 45 minutes, adding more water if required.
Remove from the heat and leave to cool. Then add the eggs and the yolks, 2 tablespoons of grated Parmesan cheese, a little finely chopped garlic and parsley and a sprinkle of grated lemon zest.
In the meantime, cut the Tuscan bread into very thin slices and add just enough to the mixture to make a sufficiently stiff paste.
Shape into not too large meatballs. Fry on one side in extra virgin olive oil in a large frying pan, then turn off the heat.
When the meatballs have cooled, brown them on the other side.
Can be eaten either hot or cold.

78.

Rane piccanti in guazzetto - *Frogs in Spicy Sauce*
Florence / Prato / Pistoia

Ingredients:

16 frogs, already cleaned
250 g peeled tomatoes
1 clove garlic
carrot, onion and celery
flour
½ glass white wine
chilli pepper
Tuscan bread
olive oil
salt

Finely chop the carrot, onion and celery and sauté in a pan with the peeled and squashed garlic clove in four tablespoons of oil.

Add the frogs and let them brown for a few minutes. Pour in the wine and let it evaporate. Add the peeled tomatoes chopped into chunks and the pinch of chilli pepper and cook for about fifteen minutes.

Serve on slices of toasted bread adding another pinch of chilli pepper.

Frogs generally live in stagnant water, but the ones used as food are caught where the water is clear and they have soft, white flesh. The meat has a delicate flavour and so it is pointless to resort to unnecessary marinades. The meat is also lean and rich in protein. Indeed, we have included them among our 'rude' recipes only because certain squeamish palates refuse to even contemplate consuming these cute little amphibians, but we can assure you from personal experience that they constitute a most sumptuous treat. Light, delicate and highly sophisticated.

79.
Ranocchi fritti - *Fried Frog Legs*
Florence / Prato / Pistoia

Ingredients:

32 frog legs
flour
2 eggs
10 cl milk
salt
oil for frying

Beat the eggs in a bowl with a pinch of salt and 10 cl of milk.
Wash and dry the frog legs, then coat them in flour and drop into the batter and leave them for fifteen minutes.
Fry in plenty of hot oil and serve accompanied by slices of lemon and another sprinkle of salt if necessary.
Cornmeal can be used for the batter instead of white flour, or a 50/50 blend of the two.

In the past, frogs were used to make a delicate soup that was considered so wholesome that an enterprising company decided to produce a tinned version.

Peeping Frog (ed. G. Kearsley, Fleet Street, London 1801).

80.

Rigaglie di pollo alla contadina – *Country Style Chicken Giblets*
Siena / Pisa

Ingredients:

> 700 g chicken giblets (livers, hearts, gizzards)
> 1 clove garlic
> sage
> ½ glass vin santo (or dessert wine)
> ½ glass white wine
> 40 g butter
> 1 tablespoon flour
> olive oil
> salt and pepper

Clean the hearts and the gizzards and chop into pieces.

Sweat the garlic and a few leaves of sage in two tablespoons of oil and the butter, then add the hearts and the gizzards and sauté for a few minutes. Pour in half a glass of white wine and let it evaporate.

Remove the hearts and the gizzards, chop them roughly then put them back in the pot. Add the cleaned livers cut into small pieces.

Continue sautéing, season with salt and pepper and sprinkle in a tablespoon of flour, then pour in half a glass of vin santo and cook for another ten minutes.

Serve the giblets in their sauce.

Chicken giblets are known in Italian as 'rigaglie', a term that derives from the medieval Latin 'regalìa' meaning fit for a king. The English term 'regalia' derives from the same root, and has preserved the meaning of royal rights and prerogatives and, by extension, the symbols and paraphernalia indicating royal status.

81.
Rognoni al vino bianco – *Kidneys in White Wine*
Florence / Arezzo

Ingredients:

700 g veal kidneys
parsley
1 glass white wine
bunch of mixed herbs
olive oil
salt and pepper

Start the day before. Clean the kidneys thoroughly, split them open and snip off the gristly inside fat under cold running water.
Place them in a bowl to marinate in the white wine with the bunch of herbs, cover the bowl and leave it in the fridge overnight.
The next day, rinse the kidneys and cut them into slices. Place them in a pot and cover them with salt and then with boiling water.
Wait until the water has cooled and then drain. Place the kidney slices in a non-stick frying pan over a low heat and, when they have released their juices, drain again.
Brown the slices for a few minutes in a pan with four tablespoons of oil, then pour over a glass of white wine. Cook over a lively heat to let the wine evaporate. When cooking is complete, add some freshly chopped parsley.

Kidneys are effectively pretty high up on the list of nasty bits and the distinctly ammonia-like smell can be fairly off-putting. Nevertheless, when fresh and well-prepared they are truly delicious.
When cleaning or marinating, always remember to use cold liquids to avoid 'cooking' the food ahead of time.

82.

Rosticciana alle olive nere – *Pork Ribs with Black Olives*
Lucca / Siena

Ingredients:

1.2 kg pork ribs
250 g tomato sauce
100 g black olives
1 clove garlic
sage
rosemary
olive oil
salt and pepper

Cut the ribs lengthwise so they are quite short and then separate them one by one.

In a large pan, sauté the peeled and squashed garlic clove in two tablespoons of olive oil with a little sage and rosemary.

Add the ribs and brown them, then drain off the excess fat – although for a wickedly greasy flavour it's better to retain it, just try!

Add the tomato sauce and the olives and season with salt and pepper.

Cook for about 45 minutes, or until the meat is ultra-tender.

Serve the ribs with the sauce spooned over.

As the name suggests, 'Rosticciana', or 'rostinciana', is normally grilled over a charcoal or wood fire. Nevertheless, it is also excellent in this unusual and flavoursome version.

83.
Scottiglia antica di carni miste - *Old-Style Mixed Meat Stew*
Arezzo

Ingredients:

200 g lamb
200 g rabbit
200 g duck
200 g chicken
200 g pigeon
250 g peeled tomatoes
1 glass white wine
garlic
flour
sage and rosemary
chilli pepper
olive oil
Tuscan bread
salt and pepper

Chop the various meats into chunks and coat them in flour, then sauté them in an earthenware pot with two tablespoons of extra virgin olive oil, two cloves of garlic, two chopped chilli peppers, two sprigs of rosemary and a few sage leaves. Pour over a glass of white wine and let it evaporate over a lively heat. Add the peeled tomatoes, season with salt and pepper and cook over a low heat with the lid on for around 40 minutes.
Serve piping hot in soup bowls ladled over slices of toasted Tuscan bread – rubbed with a raw garlic clove for the more intrepid!

Scottiglia, *also known as 'Cacciucco del Casentino' is a mixture of local meats, just as the Livorno speciality is a mixture of fish.*
It derives from an old custom whereby, when families got together, the head of each family would contribute a different type of meat so as to obtain a tastier final dish.

84.
Sedani ripieni alla pratese - *Stuffed Celery*
Prato

Ingredients:

8 large celery stalks
300 g minced beef
150 g minced Mortadella sausage from Prato (if possible, otherwise any Mortadella will do!)
400 g meat sauce
20 g chopped parsley
50 g grated Parmesan cheese
½ clove garlic, chopped
5 eggs – 2 are for the stuffing
50 g flour
nutmeg
olive oil
salt and pepper

Clean the celery, removing the fibrous threads from the larger stalks, and chop into pieces about 8 cm long. Blanch in boiling salted water.
Leave them to cool, covering them with a cloth with a weight on top of it to remove all the water. In the meantime, prepare the stuffing. Mix together the beef, Mortadella, parsley, Parmesan cheese, the half garlic clove and the two eggs, seasoning with salt, pepper and grated nutmeg.
When the celery stalks are cool and have released all their water, divide them into two lots. Fill half of them with the stuffing, then place the other half on top. Beat the other three eggs. Coat the stuffed celery in flour and then dip into the beaten eggs. Fry in plenty of olive oil until golden.
Heat the meat sauce in a large pan and when it begins to boil put in the fried celery pieces. Put the lid on the pan and cook over a low heat until the celery pieces have turned a nice brick-red colour.

85.

Spezzatino di cinghiale con olive e pinoli
Wild Boar Stew with Olives and Pine Kernels
Lucca / Grosseto

Ingredients for 6:
   1.5 kg wild boar meat

For the marinade:
   3 litres red table wine
   1 carrot
   1 onion
   1 celery stalk
   1 lemon
   2 cloves
   2 bay leaves
   rosemary
   juniper berries, squashed

For the stew:
   1 carrot
   1 onion
   1 celery stalk
   2-3 juniper berries, squashed
   2 cloves
   1 bay leaf
   400 g peeled tomatoes
   1 flat tablespoon tomato conserve
   30 g pine kernels
   300 g large green olives or stoned black olives
   salt, pepper or chilli pepper to taste
   olive oil

Start the evening before and put the wild boar meat – preferably cut into small pieces – in a large bowl to marinate in the red wine, with the herbs and vegetables indicated for the marinade. The next day, chop the celery, onion and carrot finely and sauté them with some oil in an aluminium or terracotta saucepan. Add the juniper berries, cloves and bay leaves.

Then add the drained wild boar and brown it until the meat is dry. At this point add the squashed peeled tomatoes and the just slightly diluted tomato concentrate and then, after a few minutes, the olives and the pine kernels. Complete cooking, adding hot stock if necessary. In total the cooking should take about two hours over a low heat.

Serve the wild boar with its sauce.

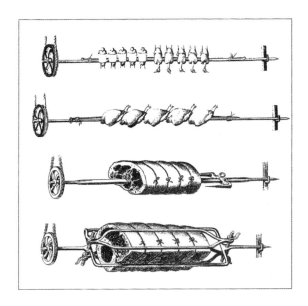

86.

Storni in tegame - *Stuffed Starlings*
Arezzo

Ingredients:

8 cleaned starlings, ready to use
200 g diced pancetta (or green bacon)
1 glass white wine
garlic
sage
rosemary
olive oil
Tuscan bread
salt and pepper

Stuff the starlings with the pancetta, a little sage and rosemary, salt and pepper. Chop the garlic, sage and rosemary finely and sauté gently in three
tablespoons of olive oil.
Add the starlings, brown them, then pour in glass of white wine and let it
evaporate. Season with salt and pepper.
Cook for around 40 minutes, adding hot stock if required.
Serve the starlings with their sauce on slices of toasted Tuscan bread.

For this recipe thrushes – which may be easier to find – can be used instead of star-
lings, following the same procedure.

87.

Stracotto alla Medici – *Medici Pot Roast*

Florence

Ingredients:

> 800 g beef shank
> 1 kg yellow potatoes (waxy not floury)
> 1 carrot
> 1 onion
> 1 celery stalk
> 2 glasses red wine
> stock
> garlic
> olive oil
> salt and pepper

Chop the carrot, onion and celery and a clove of garlic finely then sauté in a pot in three tablespoons of olive oil. Add the meat and brown it on all sides, season with salt and pepper, then pour in the red wine and a glass of stock. Put the lid on and cook over a very low heat for just under two hours.
Add the potatoes cut into large chunks and a little more salt and continue cooking for another half hour, adding more stock if required.
When it is cooked, leave the meat to cool slightly, then take it out and cut into slices and cover them with the cooking juices. Serve with the potatoes.

88.
Tegamaccio pratese - *Prato Mixed Pork Stew*
Prato

Ingredients for 6:

2 kg mixed pork (cheek, liver, lungs, sweetbreads, tongue etc.)
carrot, onion, celery
1 clove garlic
rosemary
1 tablespoon tomato conserve
olive oil
salt

Clean the various pig meat parts and chop them all into small chunks.
Chop the carrot, onion and celery finely and sauté in a pot in a little olive oil.
When the vegetables have softened, tip in the meat and add the tomato conserve diluted in a glass of warm water.
Season with salt and cook over a low heat until the sauce has condensed and the meat is soft. Add hot stock in the course of cooking if required.

Tegamaccio pratese was mostly made in the winter months when the peasants killed the pig and were able to use many different parts of the animal. The original and even ruder recipe calls for the addition of a glass of pig's blood, which similarly would have been readily available on such occasions.

89.

Testicciola alla pisana - *Pisan Boiled Lamb's Head*

Pisa

Ingredients:

2 or 3 lamb's or kid's heads
1 onion
1 carrot
1 celery stalk
1 tablespoon of capers
30 g pickles
olive oil
salt and pepper

The *strascino* was a typical street vendor who offered meat of poor quality. Etching from 1740, copy of a print by Annibale Carracci (1560-1609).

Purchase the heads already cut into pieces and boil them in salted water with the chopped vegetables for about two hours, or until the meat falls off the bones.

Let the meat cool in its stock.

Bone the meat and cut it into thin strips.

Tip it into a bowl and garnish with a mixture of chopped capers and pickles and a little extra virgin olive oil and season generously with salt and pepper.

90.
Trippa di San Frediano - *San Frediano Tripe*
Florence

Ingredients:

1 kg ready-cooked tripe
300 g peeled tomatoes
3 bay leaves
½ glass olive oil
1 celery stalk
1 carrot
1 onion
½ glass red wine
100 g Parmesan cheese
1 clove garlic
black pepper
salt

Cut the tripe into thin strips, wash it under cold running water and leave it to drain in a colander.
Peel the carrot and cut it into very thin slices lengthwise then dice.
Wash the celery stalk and remove the stringy outside filament. Divide in half lengthwise, then dice this too. Peel the onion, divide in two and chop into small cubes.
Tip the vegetables into a saucepan and sweat gently in oil, then add the bay leaves and a clove of garlic.
Sauté over a low heat for just 5 minutes, mixing every so often with a wooden spoon. Remove the garlic clove and then add the tripe and toss everything together.
Pour in the red wine and let it evaporate completely. Then add the peeled tomatoes and season with salt and pepper to taste. Put the lid on the saucepan and finish cooking the tripe, stirring frequently and adding a little hot stock from time to time. It takes about two hours.

When the tripe is cooked, sprinkle with Parmesan cheese and leave to sit for five minutes.
Serve the tripe hot, accompanied by slices of toasted bread.

Tripe is made from the different chambers of a cow's stomach known as rumen, reticulum and omasum. It can be prepared in various ways, with or without sauce.

Tripe-seller in an engraving by Francesco Curti.

91.
Zampa al sugo - *Calf's Feet in Sauce*
Florence / Prato / Pistoia

Ingredients:

4 calf's feet, ready to use
carrot, onion and celery
2 onions
5 ripe tomatoes
40 g butter
2 eggs
30 g grated Parmesan cheese
olive oil
salt and pepper

Clean the calf's feet and boil them in a pot with the chopped carrot, onion and celery in boiling salted water for about two hours, then leave them to cool in the pot.
Remove the bones and cut the meat into slices.
Chop the onion and sauté it in two tablespoons of oil and the butter. As soon as it has turned soft, add the meat. Season with salt and pepper and cook for about twenty minutes.
Peel the tomatoes and chop them into pieces, then add to the pot. Continue cooking for about another twenty minutes.
At the end, add the yolks of the two eggs and the grated Parmesan cheese.
Serve the calf's feet with another sprinkle of grated Parmesan.

SWEETS AND DESSERTS

Previous page: a satirical vignette by Giuseppe Novello, from *Il signore di buona famiglia* (Mondadori 1942). 'The Wedding Feast was cancelled ... but it wasn't possible to countermand the ice-cream for twenty-four.'

92.

Biscotti di Prato con vin santo - *Prato Biscuits with Vin Santo*
Prato

Ingredients for 8:

600 g plain or all-purpose flour
300 g sugar
150 g shelled almonds
3 eggs
2 egg yolks
a little milk
1 sachet baking powder (10 g)
1 pinch salt

Beat two eggs and the two yolks with the sugar and a drop of milk.
Add the sifted flour, the baking powder and a pinch of salt.
Toast the almonds, leave them to cool and then stir them into the mixture.
Form the paste into strips about three fingers in width and one and half fingers high.
Place them on a well-greased baking tray and brush them with beaten egg.
Bake in a pre-heated oven at 180°C for around twenty minutes.
Remove from the oven, and cut diagonally into slices about one finger thick to obtain the classic shape of biscotti di Prato (also known as cantucci).
Replace in the oven at 200°C for around 8 to 10 minutes. Remove and leave to cool.
Serve with a glass of vin santo (or dessert wine), which is used to dunk the biscuits in!

93.

Castagnaccio - *Chestnut Cake*
Florence / Lucca

Ingredients:

500 g sweet chestnut flour
30 g shelled pine kernels
8 walnuts
rosemary
olive oil
salt

Sieve the flour into a bowl and add a pinch of salt. Mix gently with a whisk
to prevent lumps forming and then add 600 cl of warm water.

Mix thoroughly until you have a smooth liquid paste, then set aside to rest
for about an hour.

Grease a low-sided baking tin and pour in the batter, making sure that it is
not more than one and a half centimetres high.

Sprinkle a few leaves of rosemary, the pine kernels and the shelled walnuts
broken into pieces over the top. Finish with a light trickle of olive oil then
bake in a pre-heated oven at 200°C for about 45 minutes.

*This is an ancient sweetmeat, originating in the Tuscan countryside in the sixteenth
century. It was very simple to make, using the chestnut flour that was widely available,
mixed with water. The result was both delicious and nutritious, and the recipe rapidly
spread throughout the mountainous areas of central Italy, being enriched along the
way by the addition of pine kernels and sometimes raisins and walnuts.*

94.
Cenci fritti - *Fried Cenci*
Florence

Ingredients:

300 g plain or all-purpose flour
60 g sugar
2 eggs
olive oil
corn oil for frying
vin santo (or dessert wine)
lemon zest
1 pinch salt
icing sugar

Mix the flour with the eggs, the sugar, 3 tablespoons of olive oil, a glass of vin santo, a little grated lemon zest and a pinch of salt.
Blend the ingredients together until you have a smooth, even paste.
Form into a ball, cover and leave to rest in the fridge for an hour.
When the time is up, roll the pastry out quite thin with a rolling pin, then cut it into fairly wide strips and then crosswise into lozenges.
Deep fry in plenty of oil and then lay on a tray lined with absorbent paper and sprinkle with icing sugar.
Serve the cenci while they are still hot.

In Tuscany, cenci are usually prepared and eaten to celebrate Carnival. The name derives from the word 'cencio' , meaning rag, and refers to their appearance.

95.

Frittelle dolci di riso della nonna Eda
Grandma Eda's Sweet Rice Fritters
Florence

Ingredients for 6:

500 g pudding rice
1 ½ litres milk
10 egg yolks
700 g sugar
1.5 g vanilla powder
3 tablespoons vin santo (or dessert wine)
grated zest of 5 oranges
grated zest of 1 lemon
1 litre seed oil (sunflower, groundnut, linseed etc.) for frying
1 pinch salt
icing sugar

Start the evening before. Put the rice in a large saucepan with one and a half litres of cold water and a pinch of salt. Bring to the boil and cook, adding the milk when it is boiling.

Stirring all the time with a wooden spoon, add the sugar and the vanilla powder half way through cooking.

At the end, the rice mixture should be very stiff. Leave to cool and put in the fridge overnight.

The next day, add the vin santo and the grated orange and lemon zest to the mixture along with the beaten egg yolks.

Mix thoroughly and if the mixture is not stiff enough you can add a little flour, but do this just before you start frying.

With the help of a tablespoon, form round fritters of about half the size of an egg and fry in plenty of boiling oil.

The fritters can be eaten hot or cold with a dusting of icing sugar.

96.
Frittelle di mele - *Apple Fritters*
Lucca / Prato / Massa Carrara

Ingredients:

2 eggs
200 g flour
100 cl milk
25 g sugar
sugar to sprinkle
vin santo (or dessert wine)
3 Golden Delicious type apples
sunflower seed oil

Prepare a batter with the eggs, flour, milk, sugar and vin santo.
Peel the apples, remove the seeds and cut them into rings.
Dip them into the batter and fry in plenty of hot sunflower seed oil.
Remove with a slotted spoon, drain and place on a tray lined with absorbent paper.
Serve with a sprinkle of granulated sugar.

97.

Necci con la ricotta - *Chestnut Pancakes with Ricotta*
Lucca

Ingredients:

> 400 g chestnut flour
> warm water
> 1 pinch salt
> 1 teaspoon sugar
> 500 g Ricotta cheese
> chestnut leaves

In a bowl, mix the chestnut flour with the sugar and a pinch of salt. Gradually add warm water and mix well until you have a smooth, dense batter. The traditional way of cooking the necci is using special sandstone discs known as testi. These are heated up over a wood fire and then a chestnut leaf is placed on top of the first testo, followed by a ladleful of batter, then another chestnut leaf, and then another very hot testo. The process then continues until a pile is formed. After two or three minutes the necci are cooked, after which they are removed from the fire and left to cool a little.
Place a tablespoon of Ricotta cheese inside each pancake and roll it up.

Obviously, since you are unlikely to have 'testi', and very probably a wood fire either, the pancakes can also be cooked one at a time on a cast-iron skillet or a nonstick frying pan, cooking for a few minutes and flipping over half-way through. Traditionally, the chestnut leaves were used both to stop the batter sticking to the pan and to give the pancake a very particular flavour. The leaves were gathered in summer and stored, then they were steeped in water for around an hour before use.

98.
Schiaccia briaca – *Tipsy Fruit and Nut Cake*
Livorno

Ingredients for 6:

1 kg white flour
500 g sugar
200 g raisins
300 g chopped nuts (walnuts, almonds, hazelnuts, pine kernels)
2 glasses oil
Aleatico to taste (or similar dessert wine)
1 glass Alchermes (liqueur)
1 knob of fresh brewers' yeast

Start the evening before. Dilute the yeast in a glass of tepid water and mix with 100 g flour. form into a ball and leave to rise overnight in a bowl covered with a cloth.
Steep the raisins in warm water.
The next day, tip the rest of the flour onto a pastry board and add the risen bread dough, the chopped nuts, the drained raisins, the oil, the Aleatico and the Alchermes.
Work everything together, kneading thoroughly and at length until you have a smooth, soft dough. Oil a round baking tin and line it with greaseproof paper, making sure that the rim is also covered. Brush the paper with oil too and then place the dough inside, stretching it so that it fills the tin. Sprinkle with pine kernels and then bake in a hot oven for 40/45 minutes. Remove from the oven and leave to cool, then put it on a plate without removing the paper it was baked on.

Cooking equipment and utensils illustrated in the plates of the *Opera* by the cook Bartolomeo Scappi (Venice, 1570).

99.

Schiacciata con l'uva - *Tuscan Grape Foccaccia*
Florence / Siena

Ingredients:

500 g plain or all-purpose flour
6 tablespoons sugar
½ glass olive oil
rosemary
25 g fresh yeast
1 kg red Canaiolo grapes (or other red wine grapes)
1 pinch salt

Dissolve the yeast in a glass of warm water, then mix it with the flour along with a trickle of oil, a teaspoon of sugar and a pinch of salt.
Knead thoroughly, then leave to rise for about two hours.
In the meantime, heat up the extra virgin olive oil in a small pan with a sprig of rosemary.
When the time is up, knock down the bread dough and knead in the fried oil and two tablespoons of sugar. Divide the dough into two equal parts.
Grease a rectangular baking tray and spread out half the dough, then sprinkle over almost all the grapes, keeping a few aside for decoration. Sprinkle two tablespoons of sugar over the grapes and finish with a trickle of oil.
Cover with the remaining dough and decorate the top with the remaining grapes. Sprinkle over another two tablespoons of sugar and finish with another trickle of oil.
Bake in a pre-heated oven at 200°C for around half an hour.

The schiacciata con l'uva is generally made in the autumn, at the time of the grape harvest, between September and October. This recipe is the most traditional one, and has its roots in the rural culture of Tuscany. In other areas it is sometimes made using white grapes, or even raisins.

100.

Torta coi becchi al cioccolato – *Peaked Chocolate Tart*

Lucca

Ingredients:

For the shortcrust pastry:
    250 g plain or all-purpose flour
    125 g butter
    125 g sugar
    1 sachet vanilla powder (10 g)
    ½ sachet baking powder (5 g)
    2 eggs
    1 pinch salt

For the filling:
    180 g sugar
    100 g flour
    6 eggs
    70 g cocoa powder
    20 cl brandy
    ½ litre milk

Prepare the pastry. Tip the flour onto a pastry board and place the softened butter and the sugar in the centre. Rub gently together and then add the sifted vanilla powder and baking powder. Continue to mix together then add the eggs and work until you have a smooth ball of pastry. Place it in the fridge for about 30 minutes.

Make the filling. In a small pot mix together the eggs, sugar and flour. Heat the milk and pour into the pot, stirring rapidly with a wooden spoon, then place the pot over a low heat. When the custard has thickened, remove from the heat and add the cocoa and the brandy. Continue stirring until you have a smooth cream.

Grease a cake tin with butter. Sprinkle a little white flour on the pastry board and roll out the pastry. Cut out a ring large enough to cover the tin including the sides and the rim, with a little overlap. Fill the pastry case with the chocolate cream. Cut the leftover pieces of pastry into strips and arrange them in a criss-cross pattern on the top of the filling.

With the tip of a knife cut the pastry on the rim diagonally at regular intervals, rolling each strip back on itself to form little rolls around the inner rim of the tin, then pull up the ends of the rolls to create the characteristic pointed 'peaks'

Bake in a pre-heated oven at 220°C for about 45 minutes or until the pastry has turned a nice hazelnut colour. Remove the tart from the tin and leave it to cool on a large serving plate.

Serve accompanied by a slightly cooled vin santo from the Lucca hills, or another dessert wine of your choice.

Not to be confused with the 'Torta coi bischeri', which has the same peaked triangular decoration around the edges — here alternatively termed 'bischeri' — but has an even richer filling that includes rice, pine kernels and raisins, as well as chocolate.

Long live the lardo!

This recipe book doesn't include only preparations belonging to traditional Tuscan cooking, but also contains original Tuscan dishes and some that come from the recipes of our own families. We could even have included some delicacies that are nowadays considered unacceptable because they feature among the ingredients fauna that are now deemed to be protected but are nevertheless an integral part of Tuscan gastronomical culture. No one would attempt to deny the fact that, until quite recently, it was still possible to eat dishes such as turtle soup, a very special delicacy especially in the Argentario where the turtles were subjected to atrocious tortures before being cooked. Similarly, in the area of Livorno and in the islands of the Tuscan archipelago, it was common to find omelettes with sea anemones, these too now listed as protected fauna. The peasants and hunters of yesteryear had no qualms about killing porcupines and hedgehogs, which they then got their wives to prepare in a way very similar to that used for wild boar, most often in the form of a sauce made after lengthy marinating of the meat. The result has been recorded by many as exquisitely flavoursome.

Obviously, we would not be so brazenly rude as to cite such recipes except in terms of historical and anthropological curiosity. We firmly believe that one can never be too sensitive, except when such sentiment veers towards prejudice and persecution. We are also convinced that this book can stimulate exchange and debate between different philosophies, ideologies and dietologies, possibly fostering some conversions along the culinary road to Damascus in one direction or the other: from soya to lardo or vice-versa.

It goes without saying that we'll be rooting for the lardo!

Nineteenth century: the first Italian 'industrial' sausage machines.

Bilingual Ingredients Index

(by recipe number)

Index of Recipes by Province

(by recipe number)

The Florentine beefsteak in a satirical illustration by Giuseppe Novello: 'Tuscan Cuisine is fine and delicate' (P. Monelli, *Il ghiottone errante*, 1935).

General Index

Printed by
POLISTAMPA FLORENCE srl
February 2024